Editor
Dawn M. Poole, Ph.D.

Editorial Manager
Elizabeth Morris, Ph.D.

Editor-in-Chief
Sharon Coan, M.S. Ed.

Illustrator
Karon Walstad

Cover Artist
Denice Adorno

Art Coordinator
Kevin Barnes

Imaging
Alfred Lau
James Edward Grace

Product Manager
Phil Garcia

Publisher
Mary D. Smith, M.S. Ed.

Step-by-Step SPREADSHEET ACTIVITIES for MICROSOFT EXCEL

Grades 4-8

D1281628

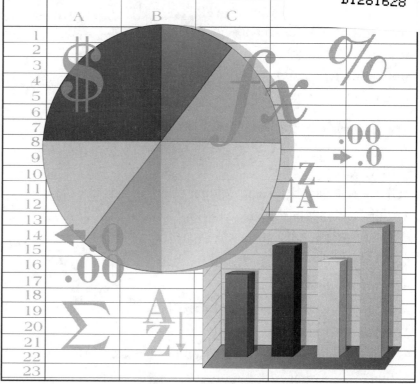

Author

Joan Marie Brown, M.A.

Teacher Created Resources, Inc.
6421 Industry Way
Westminster, CA 92683
www.teachercreated.com

ISBN: 978-0-7439-3469-5

©*2001 Teacher Created Resources, Inc.*
Reprinted, 2008
Made in U.S.A.

Table of Contents

Introduction

Microsoft Excel is a popular spreadsheet program that is used in homes, businesses, and schools. Many people often overlook the value–as well as the simplicity–of spreadsheet programs. Spreadsheets can be used to keep track of student grades, maintain budget information, and solve mathematical problems. A spreadsheet can be used anytime calculations need to be performed.

In this book, you will learn about working with spreadsheets in the *Microsoft Excel* program. Though all spreadsheet programs are similar, there are some features and processes unique to each. The thirty activities will familiarize you with creating spreadsheets from scratch, manipulating information in a spreadsheet, changing the layout and format of a spreadsheet, inserting formulas into a spreadsheet, and creating charts and graphs of information contained within a spreadsheet file.

If you are new to spreadsheets, it is recommended that you work through the activities in order, especially Activity 1. Doing so will provide you with opportunities to learn about the various menu items and features of *Microsoft Excel*. In addition, Activity 1 also walks you through some basic features of the Windows operating system. Beginning with Activity 2, you will create specific spreadsheets that apply new skills. If you are using a Macintosh operating system, the features of *Microsoft Excel* are nearly identical to what is written and shown in this book.

Many of the activities include questions that are designed to help you think about <u>why</u> the spreadsheet responds as it does. Space is provided on which to respond to the questions. Correct answers are provided in the back of the book.

<u>Notation</u>

Throughout the book, menu items are referred to in **BOLD CAPITALS**.

Commands that are found within one of these menus are written in ***Bold Italics***.

Buttons or other selections that need to be clicked are written in **Bold**.

When you are asked to type something into the spreadsheet, it will be noted in *italics* in the text.

When you are asked to press a specific key, it will be indicated inside < >. Example: Press <Enter>.

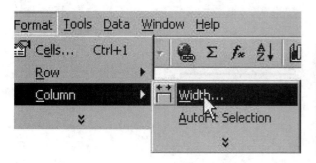 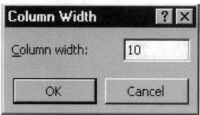

The screen shot above is written in the text like this:

Go to **FORMAT**, select ***Column*** and then choose ***Width*** from the right menu. Type *10* in the column width box. Click **OK**.

About the CD-ROM

The accompanying CD-ROM contains several templates that correspond to the book's activities. It does not contain the *Microsoft Excel* software program; *Excel* must already be installed on your computer. There is a copy of each of the book's thirty activities on the CD-ROM for comparison purposes. In several cases, an activity will begin by asking you to open a file created in a previous activity. If you have not completed the previous activity, you can simply open the file from the CD-ROM.

1. To access the CD-ROM materials, go to your Desktop and click **MY COMPUTER**.

2. One of the icons will be a CD-ROM. On most computers it is either drive D or E.

3. Double-click this icon. You will then see a list of files that are available on the CD-ROM. Double-click the one you would like to open. That action will first open *Microsoft Excel* and then open the specific file.

The materials on the CD-ROM are labeled sequentially by activity number.

Activity 1: Learn About Spreadsheets

<u>Overview</u>: This activity familiarizes you with spreadsheet vocabulary that will be used throughout the book. It also helps you to understand how to create new spreadsheets, open existing spreadsheets, and save spreadsheet files.

A spreadsheet program is a computer application used to organize, calculate and manipulate numerical data.

Opening a New Spreadsheet Workbook

A. Click the Start button in the lower-left corner of the screen.

B. Select *Programs* and the off to the right, choose *Microsoft Excel*.

When you open *Excel*, you open a new workbook. A new workbook file contains three empty worksheets, also called sheets. The names of these worksheets appear on tabs at the bottom of the workbook screen. These tabs are labeled Sheet 1, Sheet 2, and Sheet 3. Sheet 1 is the active spreadsheet, but you can switch between multiple sheets just by clicking the desired tab. More sheets can be added to any workbook, and the default of three sheets can be changed if you go to **TOOLS** and select *Preferences*.

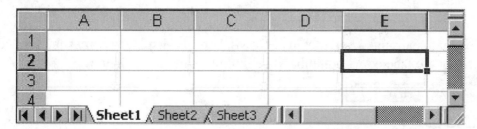

For every activity in this book, you will use Sheet 1 in the workbook to complete the exercise.

Activity 1: Learn About Spreadsheets *(cont.)*

The Spreadsheet Grid

When you look at a spreadsheet screen, you see a grid made up of columns, rows and cells.

Column

A column contains information that is arranged vertically. Column labels are displayed across the top of the spreadsheet screen; they are labeled with letters, beginning with the letter A.

	A	B	C
1			
2			
3	Column A	Column B	Column C

A. Hold the <CTRL> key and the right-arrow key on the keyboard to move all the way to the right end of the spreadsheet. What letter label does the last column have? _____

   This translates to 230 columns.

B. You can add additional columns to the spreadsheet. First, click the column label that you would like to slide to the right to make room for the new column.

	A	B	C	D
1				
2				
3	Column A	Column B	Column C	

C. Next, go to **INSERT** and select *Columns*.

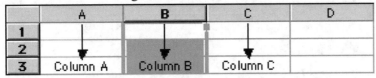

D. This will add a new column to your spreadsheet, preserving what you had already created.

	A	B	C	D
1				
2				
3	Column A		Column B	Column C

E. To delete an existing column, click on the letter of the column you would like to delete. Then go to **EDIT** and select *Delete*.

Row

A row contains information that is arranged horizontally. Row labels are displayed across the left side of the spreadsheet screen; they are labeled with numbers, beginning with the number 1.

	A	B	C
1			Row 1
2			Row 2
3			Row 3

Activity 1: Learn About Spreadsheets *(cont.)*

A. Hold the <CTRL> key and the down-arrow key on the keyboard to move all the way to the right end of the spreadsheet. How many rows does your spreadsheet file have? _____

B. Like columns, you can add additional rows to your spreadsheet. Click the row label (the number) where you would like a new row to be placed. Then go to **INSERT** and select *Rows*. Delete rows by clicking the row number you would like to delete. Then go to **EDIT** and select *Delete*.

Cell

A cell is a box in which a column and a row intersect. Each cell in a spreadsheet grid has a name or address based on its location. The first cell in a spreadsheet grid is called A1. Note that the column letter is first and the row number is second. Cell labels are not case sensitive.

	A	B	C
1	A1	B1	C1
2	A2	B2	C2
3	A3	B3	C3

Active Cell and Active Cell Address

A spreadsheet always has one active cell. The active cell is the cell in which the user has clicked. It is outlined in the computer's outline color. The address of this active cell is always displayed in the active cell address area, as indicated in the diagram below.

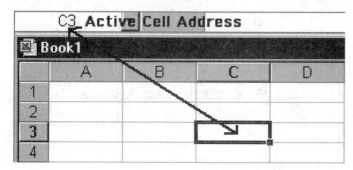

A. Click cell E5 (you may need to use one or both scroll bars to get to E5). Observe how the active cell address area displays the cell label, E5.

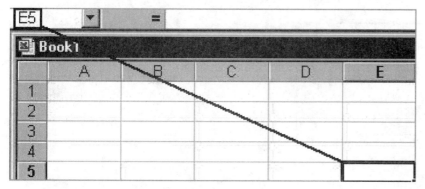

B. Click the last cell of this spreadsheet file. To get there, hold the <CTRL> key and then click the down arrow and the right arrow on the keyboard. What is the address of this cell? _____
This means there are 30 x 65,536 or 15,073,280 cells in the spreadsheet.

Activity 1: Learn About Spreadsheets *(cont.)*

Entry Bar

Click cell A1. You can get there by pressing <F5> and then typing *A1* in the **Go To** box. Once A1 is selected, type *150*. Press <Enter>. Click cell A1 again. Now look above the B in column B. Above the column labels, you see the active cell address box, four symbols, and then a white box that now contains the number 150. This white box is called the Entry Bar.

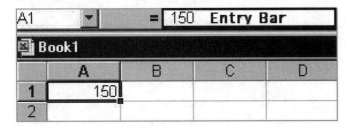

1. A. Click the Entry Bar. Use <Delete> or <Backspace> to erase 150. Now type *1234*. Press <Tab>. Click cell A1.

   B. What number is in cell A1? _____

   C. What number is in the Entry Bar? _____

2. A. Click cell A1. Click on the Entry Bar. Use <Delete> or <Backspace> to erase 1234. Now type *HI*. Press <Enter>. Click cell A1.

   B. What do you see in cell A1? _____

   C. What do you see in the Entry Bar? _____

You can type numbers, labels (words), and formulas into cells. Press <Enter> after inputting a number, label, or formula. The Entry Bar allows you to edit anything that you have typed into a cell.

Saving the Spreadsheet File

1. Go to **FILE** and select *Save*.

2. You will see a window that lists the various locations to which the file could be saved. You may choose to save to the floppy disk (drive A), hard drive (drive C), or other storage locations that will be labeled.

3. At **File Name**, type *SS Act 1*.

4. Click **SAVE**.

5. Go to **FILE** and select *Exit* (otherwise, click the X in the upper-right corner of the screen).

Activity 1: Learn About Spreadsheets *(cont.)*

Retrieving an Existing File

1. Double-click on the **My Computer** icon from the desktop.

2. Click the drive on which you saved your document.

3. Use the scroll bars to find the file called *SS Act 1*. Click this item and then click **Open**.

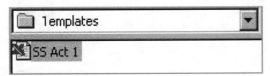

Activity 1: Time to Review

Let's find out how much you know about spreadsheets. Choose one of these activities to complete. After finishing, check your responses with those written on page 88.

Activity A

Write a letter to a person who is unfamiliar with spreadsheets. Using all of the words from the list below, explain to this person what a spreadsheet is. Make sure you use each word correctly. Underline each word as you use it. See if you can complete this activity without copying key phrases and sentences from this book.

Activity B

Create a fill-in-the-blanks worksheet. Include all of the words from the list below in the worksheet. See if you can complete this activity without copying key phrases and sentences from this book.

The Word List

Excel	spreadsheet program
workbook	worksheet
column	row
cell	grid
active cell	Entry Bar
cell address	formula
number	save
label	

Activity 2: Simple Formulas

Overview: In this activity, you will create a spreadsheet file that contains several format features as well as simple formulas. You will also print the spreadsheet file with and without the formulas displayed. This is an excellent activity to familiarize you with features of spreadsheets that will be referred to repeatedly throughout the book.

1. Open a new spreadsheet workbook. Click the **Start** button. Then select *Programs* and *Microsoft Excel*.

2. Setting Views
   A. Go to **VIEW**.
   B. Make sure there is a check in front of *Formula Bar*.
   C. Be sure that *Normal* is selected from this menu.
   D. Click *Customize*. A Customize window will open. Click the **Options** tab. Remove the check that is to the left of "Menus show recently used commands first." Click **Close**. You want to turn off this menu item so that whenever you pull down a menu, all of the commands will be displayed instead of only those that were used recently.

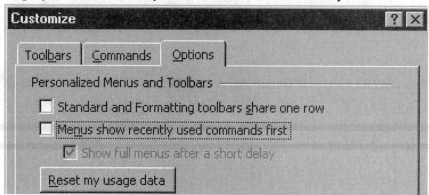

   E. Go to **VIEW**. Be sure there is a check in front of *Standard* and *Formatting*. The Standard Toolbar includes buttons for some of the most common tasks that are performed in *Excel*, such as saving, printing, spell-checking, and others.

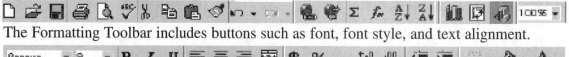

   The Formatting Toolbar includes buttons such as font, font style, and text alignment.

   F. Be sure that the magnification is set to 100% so that you can easily read the spreadsheet data.

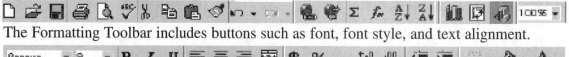

3. Entering Data

   A. Set up your spreadsheet file so it looks exactly like the one below.

	A	B	C	D	E
1				The Answers	
2	Add	389	14		
3	Subtract	936	257		
4	Multiply	450	8		
5	Divide	278100	300		

Activity 2: Simple Formulas *(cont.)*

    B. To erase a mistake, click the cell and then press <Delete> <u>OR</u> go to **EDIT**, select *Clear*, and then choose **Contents**.

4. Changing the Spreadsheet Format
    A. Click the **Select All** button, located in the upper-left corner of the spreadsheet window.

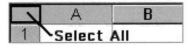

    This action selects every cell in Sheet 1; any formatting that is applied will be applied to the entire spreadsheet.
    B. Go to **FORMAT**. Choose *Row*, *Autofit*.
    C. Go to **FORMAT**. Choose *Column*, *Width*. Type <15>. Click **OK**.
    D. Go to **FORMAT**. Choose *Cells*. Click the **Font** tab. Choose **Arial**, **Regular**, **12**; click **OK.**
    E. Within the *Cells* window, click the **Alignment** tab. At **Text Alignment**, **Horizontal**, click the arrow and select **Right**. Click **OK.**

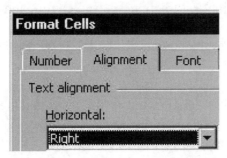

    You can instead click one of the alignment buttons in the Formatting Toolbar to right-align.

5. Adding Borders
    A. Click cell A2 and drag through A5 to select that range of cells. The spreadsheet will look like this after you make the selection.

	A	B
1		
2	Add	389
3	Subtract	936
4	Multiply	450
5	Divide	278100

    B. Click the **B** on the Format Toolbar to bold those labels.
    C. Click the border icon in the Format Toolbar. A border palette will appear below the icon. Choose the right border icon.

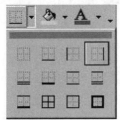

Activity 2: Simple Formulas *(cont.)*

    D. Click cell D2 and drag through D5. Add a left border to this column using the left border icon in the border palette.

	A	B	C	D
1				The Answers
2	**Add**	389	14	
3	**Subtract**	936	257	
4	**Multiply**	450	8	
5	**Divide**	278100	300	

    E. After making all of these changes, your spreadsheet should look like this.

6. About Simple Formulas
   - A formula is a set of computational instructions. The spreadsheet program carries out these computations and displays the results in a designated cell.
   - In a spreadsheet, a formula always begins with an equal sign (=). The formula also specifies the cells and/or numbers that should be included in the calculation. A formula uses one or more of the basic mathematical operations of addition, subtraction, multiplication, and division.
   - The formula =B5+C4 adds the contents of cell B5 to the contents of cell C4 and displays the sum in the cell in which the formula was typed.

7. Numeric Keypad

   Did you know that your keyboard has a numeric keypad? It is located on the far right side of the keyboard. Find the equals, plus, minus, times, and divide sign on the numeric keypad. You may choose to type these symbols and numbers using the numeric keypad or by using the traditional keyboard.

8. Let's figure out the formula that belongs in cell D2 in the spreadsheet. The formula should calculate the sum of the contents contained in cells B2 and C2.
   - A. Click cell D2.
   - B. Type =B2+C2 and <Enter>. The + and = are on the same key on the top row of the keyboard. To type the +, you need to hold the <Shift> key while clicking the +/= key.
   - C. What happened after you hit <Enter>? _____
   - D. Click cell D2. Cell D2 is holding two pieces of information–the formula and the computation. The Entry Bar displays the formula; you would click the Entry Bar to edit the formula. The answer to the computation is displayed in cell D2.

9. Let's figure out the formula that belongs in cell D3. This formula should display the difference between the contents contained in cells B3 and C3.
   - A. Click cell D3.
   - B. Type =B3-C3 and <Enter>.
   - C. What happened after you pressed <Enter>? _____

10. Let's figure out the formula that belongs in cell D4. This formula should display the product of the contents contained in cells B4 and C4.
   - A. Click cell D4.
   - B. Type =B4*C4 and <Enter>. Type the * by holding the <Shift> key while typing the number *8* or else use the * key in the numeric keypad.
   - C. What happened after you pressed <Enter>? _____

Activity 2: Simple Formulas *(cont.)*

11. Let's figure out the formula that belongs in cell D5. This formula should display the result of dividing the contents of cell B5 by the contents of cell C5.
    A. Click cell D5.
    B. Type =*B5/C5* and <Enter>. The / is on the same key as the question mark, or you may type the / key in the numeric keypad.
    C. What happened after you pressed <Enter>? _____

12. Final Formatting and Editing
    A. Add a footer to the document. Go to **VIEW** and choose *Header and Footer*. Click the **Header/Footer** tab. Click the **Custom Footer** button. In the box labeled "Left Section," type *Activity 2*, press <Enter> and type *your name*. Click **OK**.
    B. Spell-check the document. Click the **ABC** button on the Standard Toolbar.
    C. Proofread the document to check for other mistakes beyond spelling errors.
    D. Change the paper layout to landscape. Go to **FILE** and choose *Page Setup*. Click **Landscape** and then select **OK**.
    E. Go back to **FILE** and select *Page Setup*. Click the **Sheet** tab. Put a check in front of "Gridlines" and another check in front of "Row and Column Headings." Click **OK**.
    F. Save the document. Name the file *SS Act 2*. Follow the instructions on page 8 if you need assistance with the save process.

13. Print Preview
    Click the **Print Preview** icon from the Standard Toolbar <u>OR</u> go to **FILE** and select *Print Preview*. This shows what your spreadsheet will look like when printed. If there are any changes that should be made, click the **Close** button and make the changes. If you make any changes, go back to **FILE** and choose *Save*.

14. Print the Spreadsheet with Answers Displayed
    Go to **FILE** and select *Print*. Click **OK**.

15. Print the Spreadsheet with Formulas Displayed
    A. Go to **TOOLS**. Choose *Options*.
    B. Click the **View** tab. Put a check in the box in front of "Formulas." Click **OK**.
    C. Go to **FILE** and select *Print*. Click **OK**.
    D. After printing, repeat step B, except remove the check in front of Formulas.

16. Go to **FILE** and select *Exit*.

Activity 2: Time to Review

Complete these sentences. Check your responses with those on page 88.

1. A spreadsheet is _____.

2. You can type _____, _____, and _____ into cells.

3. A formula must always begin with an _____.

4. Write the formula that you would type in cell A4 to add the following cell contents.

	A
1	977
2	441
3	390
4	

_____

5. Write the formula that you would type into cell D4 to multiply the following cell contents.

	A	B	C
1	3	2	5

_____

Activity 3: Sum It!

Overview: You will learn about the SUM function, which is used to add various cells together. After learning about the function and how it works, you will have the opportunity to apply the function to a spreadsheet file.

About the SUM Function.
A spreadsheet program contains a number of pre-written formulas called functions. Functions involve calculations, so they are still considered to be formulas. Unlike formulas, however, functions are calculations that the spreadsheet already understands how to perform. All you need to do to use a function is specify the cells to which the function should be applied.

What does the SUM function do?
The SUM function automatically adds the numbers found in a specified range of cells. The cells can be selected from a column or a row.

What does the SUM function look like?
All formulas begin with an equal sign, and because SUM is also a formula, it is no exception. The function must also include a range of cells to which the calculation will be applied. An example is *=SUM(A1:A5).*

(A1:A5) is the way that the range of cells is designated. Rather than typing (A1,A2,A3,A4,A5), the colon indicates that all of the cells between the first one listed and last one listed should also be included in the calculation. The word "Sum" is not case sensitive.

How does the SUM function work?
A. To use the SUM function to find the sum of the numbers located in cells A1, A2, A3, A4, and A5, you first click the cell in which you would like the sum to be displayed. In this case, A6 might be an appropriate cell in which to display the sum. Enter the following data into a spreadsheet file, and then click cell A6.

	A
1	756
2	5678
3	234
4	87
5	567
6	

B. Next, type *=SUM(A1:A5)* and press <Enter>.

A6	▼	=	=SUM(A1:A5)

Book1

	A	B	C	D
1	756			
2	5678			
3	234			
4	87			
5	567			
6	7322			

C. You will see that the sum is displayed in cell A6 while the actual function is displayed in the Entry Bar. If you need to change the function, do so in the Entry Bar.

Activity 3: Sum It! *(cont.)*

An alternative to typing *=SUM(A1:A5)* is to click the summation button from the Standard Toolbar.
- A. Delete the contents of cell A6.
- B. Click cell A6.
- C. Click the summation button from the Standard Toolbar.

- D. The spreadsheet will try to predict what cells to add by examining where data is entered in relation to the cell in which the sum will be placed. It puts a selection rectangle around these cells so that you can verify that they are, indeed, the correct ones.

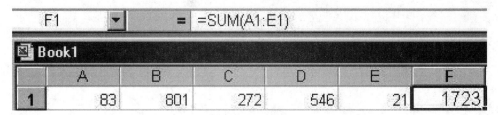

- E. If you wish to change the range that the spreadsheet program predicted, you can make the change in the Entry Bar.
- F. Press <Enter>. You will see the sum in cell A6, just as you did when you typed *=SUM(A1:A5)*.
- G. What would the function look like if you wanted to add the contents of cells B3, B4, B5, and B6?

The same function format is used to find the sum of numbers contained in a row. The only adjustment from the above function is in specifying the range of cells to which the function should be applied.

	A	B	C	D	E	F
1	83	801	272	546	21	1723

F1   = *=SUM(A1:E1)*

What would the function look like if you wanted to add the contents of cells C5, D5, E5, and F5?

Your turn to try!
1. Open a new spreadsheet file.

2. Checking Settings
   - A. Go to **VIEW**.
   - B. Make sure there is a check in front of ***Formula Bar***.
   - C. Go to ***Toolbars***. Make sure there are checks in front of ***Standard*** and ***Formatting***.
   - D. Go to ***Toolbars*** again. Click ***Customize***. Click the **Options** tab. If there is a check in front of "Menus show recently used commands first," remove it.

Activity 3: Sum It! *(cont.)*

3. Enter text and numbers into the spreadsheet file so it looks like this.

	A	B	C	D	E
1		23	1998		
2		45	3456		
3		67	2134		
4		89	5678		
5		23	3214		
6		45	8765		
7		12	9876		
8		35	2334		
9		67	1212		
10	**SUM**				

4. Right-align and bold the contents of cell A10. Click the cell and then use the appropriate buttons in the Formatting Toolbar.

5. Entering the functions
   A. Click cell B10.
   B. Type *=SUM(B1:B9)* and press <Enter> OR click the summation button from the Standard Toolbar.
   C. Click cell C10.
   D. Add the numbers in Column C. Use the SUM function or the summation button to do this.
   E. What does the function look like?
   F. Add numerical data to Columns D and E. In D10 and E10, insert the function that will provide the sum for each of these columns of data.

6. Make sure the cells containing the row sums are set to display data with no decimals. If you need to change the settings, go to **FORMAT** and select *Cells*. Click the **Number** Tab and set the number of decimals to *0*.

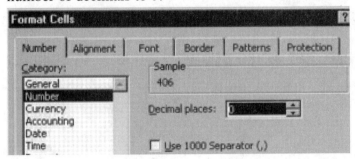

You can also click the **increase/decrease decimal** buttons from the Formatting Toolbar to make this change.

7. Add a footer to the document. Go to **VIEW** and choose *Header and Footer*. Click the **Header/Footer** tab. Click the **Custom Footer** button. In the box labeled "Center Section," type *Activity 3*, press <Enter> and type *your name*. Click **OK**.

Activity 3: Sum It! *(cont.)*

8. Save the document. Name the file *SS Act 3*. Follow the instructions on page 8 if you need to review the save process.

9. Print the spreadsheet with answers displayed. Go to **FILE** and select *Print*. Click **OK**.

10. Print the spreadsheet with formulas displayed.
    A. Go to **TOOLS**. Choose *Options*.
    B. Click the **View** tab. Put a check in the box in front of "Formulas." Click **OK**.
    C. Go to **FILE** and select *Print*. Click **OK**.

11. Go to **FILE** and select *Exit*.

Activity 3: Time to Review

Answer the following questions. Check your responses with those on page 89.

1. Instead of using the SUM function, what formula could you type that would result in the sum of the numbers in column B of your spreadsheet?

    _____

2. What is the advantage of using the SUM function over this alternative formula (from your response to question 1)?_____

    _____

3. What would the function look like that would add the contents of cells K1 through cell K250?_____

Activity 4: Fill Down

Overview: This activity teaches you how to copy a function or formula and apply it to additional cells using the Fill Down command in the spreadsheet.

1. Open a new workbook. Be sure that appropriate Toolbars and settings are selected (see page 10).

2. Set up your spreadsheet so it looks like this.

	A	B	C
1	124	421	
2	96	45	
3	3	12	
4	24	24	
5	42	3	

3. Click cell C1. Type the formula =A1+B1 and press <Enter>.

4. Cell C1 contains the formula that we want to copy into cells C2, C3, C4, and C5.

	A	B	C
1	124	421	545
2	96	45	
3	3	12	
4	24	24	
5	42	3	

A. Click cell C1.

B. Go to **EDIT** and select *Copy* OR click the **Copy** button from the Standard Toolbar.

C. Click cell C2.

D. Go to **EDIT** and select *Paste* OR click the **Paste** button from the Standard Toolbar.

E. What number appears in cell C2? _____

F. What formula appears in cell C2? _____

G. What happens each time the formula is pasted into a new row? _____

_____

5. A command called Fill can be used to copy and paste a formula or function to additional cells. The spreadsheet contains a Fill Down command and a Fill Right command. In the example above, using the Fill Down command is more efficient than retyping the addition formula into cells C2, C3, C4, and C5. It is also more efficient than repeatedly pasting the formula into these cells. The Fill Down command automatically adjusts the cell labels based on the row to which the function or formula is copied. It can make this adjustment because the pattern within the formula is what really gets duplicated.

A. Click cell C1.

B. When the cursor is inside cell C1, it is a thick cross.

	A	B	C
1	124	421	✥545
2	96	45	
3	3	12	
4	24	24	
5	42	3	

Activity 4: Fill Down *(cont.)*

If you move the cursor to the lower-right corner of cell C1, it changes to a thin cross. Position the cursor so it is a thin cross.

	A	B	C
1	124	421	545
2	96	45	
3	3	12	
4	24	24	
5	42	3	

C. Click and drag to cell C5.

	A	B	C
1	124	421	545
2	96	45	
3	3	12	
4	24	24	
5	42	3	

D. Let go of the mouse. Cells C1 through C5 should now show the sum of each row's column A and column B contents.

	A	B	C
1	124	421	545
2	96	45	141
3	3	12	15
4	24	24	48
5	42	3	45

6. Go to **TOOLS**. Choose *Options*. Click the **View** tab. Put a check in front of "Formulas." Click **OK**. Your screen should look like this.

	A	B	C
1	124	421	=A1+B1
2	96	45	=A2+B2
3	3	12	=A3+B3
4	24	24	=A4+B4
5	42	3	=A5+B5

When you copied and pasted the formula *=A1+B1* from cell C1 to cells C2, C3, C4 and C5, the formula automatically adjusted itself based on the row to which it was pasted.

    In cell C2, the formula changed to *=A2+B2*

    In cell C3, the formula changed to *=A3+B3*

    In cell C4b, the formula changed to *=A4+B4*

    In cell C5, the formula changed to *=A5+B5*

7. Insert a footer.
   A. Type *Activity 4*.
   B. Type *your name*.

8. Save this spreadsheet to your disk. Name this file *SS Act 4*.

9. Print this spreadsheet with the answers showing.

Activity 4: Fill Down *(cont.)*

10. Print this spreadsheet with the formulas displayed. Make sure all parts of the formulas can be seen; adjust column width if necessary.

11. Go to **FILE** and select *Exit*.

Activity 4: Time to Review

Answer the following questions. Check your responses with those on page 89.

1. What does the Fill Down command do? _____

   _____

2. When would you use the Fill Down command?_____

   _____

3. What adjustment automatically happens when the Fill Down command is used? _____

   _____

Activity 5: Fill Right

<u>Overview</u>: This activity teaches you how to copy a function or formula and paste it to additional cells in the same row using the Fill Right command in the spreadsheet.

1. Open a new spreadsheet file. If you need to adjust any settings from the **VIEW** menu, do so.

2. Set up your spreadsheet so it looks like this. Be sure to add the borders, bolding, and alignment as shown.

	A	B	C	D	E
1		124	421	969	48
2		6543	98765	74353	9382
3		353	543	876	3323
4	**SUM**				

3. Click cell B4. Type *=B1+B2+B3*. Press <Enter>.
   What would the function look like that produces the same answer? _____

4. Click cell B4. The Entry Bar displays the formula *= B1+B2+B3*. This is the formula that we want to copy to cells C4, D4, and E4.
   What has to change in this formula to make each calculation correct?

   _____

5. To save some time and effort, the Fill Right command will be used to copy and paste the formula to additional cells in the same row. This is more efficient than retyping the formula into B4, C4, and D4. In addition, the Fill Right command automatically adjusts the labels in the formula based on the column in which the answer is displayed.
   A. Click cell B4.
   B. Position the cursor in the lower-right corner of cell B4 so that it changes to a thin cross.

	A	B	C	D	E
1		124	421	969	48
2		6543	98765	74353	9382
3		353	543	876	3323
4	SUM	7020			

   C. Drag to cell E4 and let go.

	A	B	C	D	E
1		124	421	969	48
2		6543	98765	74353	9382
3		353	543	876	3323
4	SUM	7020	99729	76198	12753

6. Go to **TOOLS**. Choose *Options*. Click the **View** tab. Put a check in front of "Formulas." Click **OK**. Your screen should look like this.

	A	B	C	D	E
1		124	421	969	48
2		6543	98765	74353	9382
3		353	543	876	3323
4	SUM	=B1+B2+B3	=C1+C2+C3	=D1+D2+D3	=E1+E2+E3

Activity 5: Fill Right *(cont.)*

When you copied the formula =*B1+B2+B3* from cell B4 and pasted into cells C4, D4, and E4, the formula automatically adjusted itself based on the column to which it was pasted.

In cell C4, the copied formula changed to =*C1+C2+C3*
In cell D4, the copied formula changed to =*D1+D2+D3*
In cell E4, the copied formula changed to =*E1+E2+E3*

7. Insert a footer.
   A. Type *Activity 5*.
   B. Type *your name*.

8. Save the spreadsheet to your disk. Name this file *SS Act 5*.

9. Print the spreadsheet with the answers showing.

10. Print this spreadsheet with the formulas displayed.

11. Go to **FILE** and select *Exit*.

Activity 5: Time to Review

Check your answers with those on page 89.

1. What does the Fill Right command do?_____

_____

2. If you positioned the cursor in the lower-right corner of cell A1 in this diagram, and dragged the cursor to cell D1, what would the contents of cell C1 be?

	A	B	C	D
1	Fill Right			

_____

Activity 6: Back To School Shopping Trip 1

<u>Overview</u>: In this activity, you will create a spreadsheet file that calculates the total price of several purchased items. In addition, you will be asked to compute the tax on these items as well as the grand total. Simple formulas will be developed to perform the calculations. The Fill command, used in Activities 4 and 5, will be applied.

1. Open a new spreadsheet file.

2. Mrs. Smith did some back-to-school shopping in August for her three children. Below you can see the items she purchased along with the quantity and cost of each. Type the following information into the spreadsheet file. You will need to widen column A and bold row 1.

	A	B	C	D
1	**Item**	**How Many?**	**Price**	**Total**
2	Backpacks	3	8.98	
3	Pairs of Shoes	3	38.49	
4	Jackets	3	29.95	
5	Packs of Paper	6	1.19	
6	Binders	3	3.98	
7	Pens	3	2.59	
8	Erasers	3	0.69	
9	Rulers	3	0.89	

3. Cell Alignment

   A. Click cell C1 and drag through cell D1. It should look like this:

	A	B	C	D
1	Item	How Many?	Price	Total

   B. Click the right-align button from the Formatting Toolbar.

   C. Although there is currently no text in cells B10-D12, follow steps A and B to right-align those cells.

4. Formatting Currency

   A. Click the letter C at the top of column C and keep the mouse clicked while dragging to column D. This process will select the complete contents of both columns.

	A	B	C	D
1	Item	How Many?	Price	Total
2	Backpacks	3	8.98	
3	Pairs of Shoes	3	38.49	
4	Jackets	3	29.95	
5	Packs of Paper	6	1.19	
6	Binders	3	3.98	
7	Pens	3	2.59	
8	Erasers	3	0.69	
9	Rulers	3	0.89	

   B. Click the **Currency** button from the Formatting Toolbar.

   This will format the numbers in columns C and D so that they will be displayed with a dollar sign and two decimals.

Activity 6: Back To School Shopping Trip 1 *(cont.)*

5. Let's figure out how much money Mrs. Smith spent on backpacks.
   A. Click Cell D2.
   B. Type =*B2*C2*.
   C. What do you think this formula will do? _____
   D. Press <Enter>.
   E. What did this formula do? _____

6. Let's figure out how much money Mrs. Smith spent on new shoes.
   A. Click Cell D3.
   B. Type =*B3*C3*.
   C. What do you think this formula will do? _____
   D. Press <Enter>.
   E. What did this formula do? _____

7. Your turn to enter a formula.
   A. Click cell D4. Type the formula that will compute the amount Mrs. Smith spent on new jackets. Remember that all formulas begin with an equal sign. Press <Enter> after typing the formula.
   B. What formula did you type? _____

8. Filling Down
   A. Click cell D4. Position the mouse in the lower-right corner of the cell, and then drag to cell D9 to fill down.

	A	B	C	D
1	Item	How Many?	Price	Total
2	Backpacks	3	$ 8.98	$ 26.94
3	Pairs of Shoes	3	$ 38.49	$ 115.47
4	Jackets	3	$ 29.95	$ 89.85
5	Packs of Paper	6	$ 1.19	
6	Binders	3	$ 3.98	
7	Pens	3	$ 2.59	
8	Erasers	3	$ 0.69	
9	Rulers	3	$ 0.89	

   B. Click cell D6. What is the formula in this cell? _____
   C. Is this the correct formula for this cell? _____

9. Creating a Border
   A. Highlight cells A9 through D9.
   B. Click the **Bottom Border** button to create a line below this group of cells.

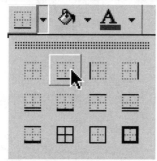

Activity 6: Back To School Shopping Trip 1 *(cont.)*

10. Computing the Subtotal
    A. Click cell C10. Type *Subtotal*.
    B. Click cell D10. Type *=D2+D3+D4+D5+D6+D7+D8+D9*.
    C. What do you think this formula will do? _____
    D. Press <Enter>.
    E. Were you correct? _____
    F. What could you have typed instead of what is printed in step 10B to perform the same calculation? _____

11. Computing the Sales Tax
    A. Click cell C11. Type *Sales Tax*.
    B. If Mrs. Smith lives in an area that has a 6% sales tax rate, what formula should be typed into cell D11 to compute the tax on the purchased items? _____
    C. Click cell D11 and type the formula you wrote in step B. Press <Enter>.
    D. If the number displayed in D11 is not $15.83, check to see where you made an error. It is possible that you incorrectly typed the price of one of the purchased items or that your sales tax formula contains an error.

12. Another Bottom Border
    A. Select cells C11 and D11.
    B. Add a bottom border to these cells.

13. Computing the Grand Total
    A. Click cell C12. Type *Grand Total*.
    B. What formula should be typed into cell D12 to compute the total of all of the purchases plus the sales tax? _____
    C. Click cell D12 and type the formula written in step B. Press <Enter>.
    D. If the number displayed in D11 is not $279.68, check to see where you made an error.

14. Finishing
    A. Click the **Select All** button.

	A
1	**Item**

    Go to **FORMAT**. Choose *Column*, *Autofit Selection*.
    B. Add a footer.
       Type *Activity 6*.
       Type *Your Name*.
    C. Spell check.
    D. Change to landscape format. Go to **FILE** and select *Page Setup*. Click **Landscape**. Click **OK**.

15. Saving and Printing
    A. Go to **FILE** and choose *Save*. Name the file *SS Act 6*. If you need help with the save process, review page 8.
    B. Print the spreadsheet with the answers displayed.
    C. Print the spreadsheet with the formulas displayed. If you need help with this process, review page 22, number 6.

16. Go to **FILE** and select *Exit*.

Activity 7: Back To School Shopping Trip 2

<u>Overview</u>: This activity helps you to understand the importance of using cell locations in a formula. You will change some of the entries in the file *SS Act 6* and observe how the spreadsheet responds to these changes. You can complete this activity using the *SS Act 6* template on the CD-ROM if you did not create your own version of the file.

1. Open the file called *SS Act 6*.

   <u>If you completed SS Act 6</u>: Find the file called *SS Act 6* on your floppy disk or hard drive. Double-click this file to open it.

   <u>If you did not create SS Act 6</u>: Insert the book's CD-ROM into the computer. Double-click the **My Computer** icon on the desktop. Then double-click the icon that represents your computer's CD-drive (depending on your computer, it could be the D- or E-drive).

   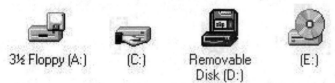

   3¼ Floppy (A:)   (C:)   Removable   (E:)
                              Disk (D:)

   Double-click the file called *SS Act 6* to open it.

2. Data Display

   You will want the display to show the contents of the cells, and not the formulas. If the formulas are displayed, go to **TOOLS**. Choose *Options*. Click the **View** tab and remove the check that is in front of "Formulas." Click **OK**.

3. Price Change

   A. What do you think will happen in cell D4 if you change the price of a jacket to $39.95?
   _____

   B. What number is displayed in cell D4 now? _____

   C. Click cell C4. Type *39.95*. Click the **B** in the Formatting Toolbar to bold the cell contents. Press <Enter>.

   D. What number is displayed in cell D4 now? _____

   E. Why did this change occur? _____

4. Quantity Change

   A. What do you think will happen in cell D5 if you change the number of packs of paper purchased to 9? _____

   B. What number is displayed in cell D5 now? _____

   C. Click cell C5. Type *9*. Click the **B** in the Formatting Toolbar to bold the cell contents. Press <Enter>.

   D. What number is displayed in cell D5 now? _____

   E. Why did this change occur? _____

5. One More Spreadsheet Change

   A. What do you think will happen to the subtotal, sales tax, and grand total if you change one of the quantities or prices in columns C or D? _____

   B. What number is displayed in cell D10 now? _____

   C. What number is displayed in cell D11 now?_____

   D. What number is displayed in cell D12 now? _____

   E. Click cell C7. Type *2.98*. Bold the cell contents. Press <Enter>.

Activity 7: Back to School Shipping Trip 2 *(cont.)*

    F. What number is displayed in cell D10 now? _____

    G. What number is displayed in cell D11 now?_____

    H. What number is displayed in cell D12 now? _____

6. Changing the Footer
    A. Go to **VIEW** and select *Header and Footer*.
    B. Replace *Activity 6* with *Activity 7*.
    C. Go to **FILE** and choose *Save*.

Activity 7: Time to Review

Answer the following questions. Check your responses with those on page 90.

1. You made several changes to this spreadsheet. Each time you made a change, some of the entries in column D changed automatically. Why?

    _____

    _____

2. If the original formula in cell D4 had been *=3*29.95*, what would have happened to the subtotal, tax, and grand total when you changed the price of a jacket?_____

    _____

    _____

Activity 8: Class Party

Overview: This activity is designed to incorporate several formulas used to figure out how much each person needs to contribute to fund a class party. You will apply concepts from Activities 6 and 7.

1. Open a new spreadsheet file.

2. Mr. James is planning a Pizza Party for his social studies class of 30 students. He wants to know how much money he should collect from each student for this party. A spreadsheet will help him with this calculation. Type the following entries into the spreadsheet file.

	A	B	C	D
1	Class Party			
2				
3	Items	How Many?	Cost Per Item	Total
4	Paper Plates			
5	Napkins			
6	Paper Cups (8 ounces)			
7	Balloons (10 per package)			
8	Pizza (10 slices per pizza)			
9	Soft Drink (64 ounce bottle)			
10	Cookies (30 per package)			
11	Large Bag of Potato Chips			
12	Large Bag of Pretzels			

3. Widening Columns
   A. Position your cursor in column A. The cursor should be a thick cross.

   B. Move the cursor to the right until it is positioned over the vertical line between columns A and B. This will change the cursor to a thin cross with arrows on the right and left.

   C. Click and drag the vertical line to the right until the column is wide enough to display all of the contents. Do the same thing in column C.

4. Right-align the contents of cells B3, C3, and D3.
   A. Click cell B3.
   B. With the mouse clicked, drag through cells C3 and D3. Your screen should look like this.

	A	B	C	D
1	Class Party			
2				
3	Items	How Many?	Cost Per Item	Total

   C. Click the **Right-Align** button in the Formatting Toolbar.

5. Right-align the contents of cells B14, C14, B15 and C15. Use the same process as in step 4 above.

Activity 8: Class Party *(cont.)*

6. More Formatting
   A. Select cells A3 through D3.
   B. Add a bottom border to these cells by clicking the **Bottom Border** button.

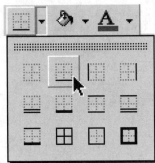

   C. Click the **Fill Color** button and select the color you would like to have fill the cells.

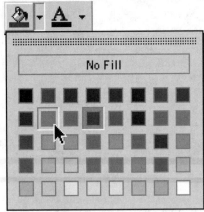

   D. Click the **Font Color** Button and select the color for the text in the cells.

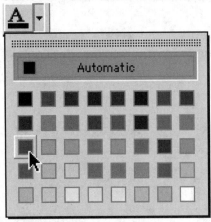

7. Formatting Numbers
   A. Select columns C and D.

	A	B	C	D
1	Class Party			
2				
3	Items	How Many?	Cost Per Item	Total
4	Paper Plates		0.10	

   B. Click the $ button from the Formatting Toolbar.

Activity 8: Class Party *(cont.)*

8. Enter estimates in column B for the number of each item needed. Remember, you are buying food for 30 hungry kids.

9. Adding More Information
   A. What formula will you use to calculate the total cost of each item? Remember to use cell locations. _____
   B. Type the formulas into Column D to compute each item total.
   C. Click cell C14. Type *Grand Total*.
   D. Click cell C15. Type *Student Contribution*.
   E. What formula will be used to calculate the Grand Total?_____
   F. Type your response to E in cell D14.
   G. Each student needs to contribute an equal amount of money toward this pizza party. What formula will calculate the amount of the individual contribution?_____
   _____
   H. Why is this the best way to build the formula?_____
   I. Type your response to G into cell D15.
   J. How is this spreadsheet helpful in figuring out individual contributions?

10. Go to **VIEW** and choose ***Header and Footer***. In the Footer, type *Activity 8* and <Enter>. Then type *your name*.

11. Print with Gridlines and Rows/Columns
    A. Go to **FILE** and select ***Page Setup***.
    B. Click the **Sheet** tab.
    C. Put a check in front of "Gridlines."
    D. Put a check in front of "Row and Column Headings."

12. Change the paper layout to landscape. Go to **FILE** and choose ***Page Setup***. Click **Landscape** and then select **OK**.

13. Go to **FILE** and select ***Save***. Name the file *SS Act 8*.

14. Print one version of the spreadsheet with just the cell content displayed. Print another copy with the formulas displayed. Compare your formulas to those included in the *SS Act 8* template on the CD-ROM.

15. Go to **FILE** and select ***Exit***.

Activity 9: Birthday Party

<u>Overview</u>: In this activity, you will use a spreadsheet file to plan for a birthday party. In the spreadsheet, you will enter party items and construct formulas that perform several calculations related to the event.

1. Open a new spreadsheet file.

2. This year, $60.00 has been budgeted for your birthday party. You will invite 11 people to this party. That means, including you, there will be a total of 12 people at the party. You decide to create a spreadsheet to keep track of party expenses. Your goal is to keep the cost of the party under $60.00 so that additional money does not need to be contributed to the party budget. Enter the information below into your spreadsheet.

	A	B	C	D
1	Birthday Party/12 Guests			
2				
3	Items	How Many?	Cost Per Item	Total
4	Dinner Plates		0.1	
5	Dessert Plates		0.05	
6	Party Napkins		0.05	
7	Party Cups (8 ounces)		0.06	
8	Balloons (10 per pack)		1.5	
9	Party Decorations (1 set)		5	
10	Pizza (10 slices per pizza)		12.95	
11	Sub Sandwich (feeds 8)		15	
12	Bottle of Soda (64 ounces)		1.99	
13	Birthday Cake (16 slices)		8	
14	Large Bag of Potato Chips		3	
15			Total	
16			Over Budget	

Reminders:
- To erase a mistake in the spreadsheet, click in the cell containing the error and press <Backspace>.
- To insert an additional row into the spreadsheet, click on the row number below where you want a row inserted. Then go to **INSERT** and choose *Rows*.
- To delete a row from the spreadsheet, select a row by clicking on the row number. Then go to **EDIT** and select *Delete*.

3. Formatting Adjustments
   A. Change the width of columns A and B so that all of the cell content is displayed.
   B. Select cells A3 through D3.
   C. Add a bottom border to these cells.
   D. Choose a fill color for these cells.
   E. Choose a font color for these cells.
   F. Select cells A14 through D14.
   G. Add a bottom border to these cells.
   H. Select cells C4 through D14.
   I. Format these cells for currency.
   J. Format D15 and D16 for currency as well.
   K. Right-align the words in cells B3, C3, and D3. Also right align cells C15 and C16.

Activity 9: Birthday Party *(cont.)*

4. In column B, enter estimates for the quantity of each item you need for the party. Remember that there will be 12 people in attendance.

5. In cells D4 through D14, enter the formulas needed to calculate the cost of each item. Be sure each formula contains cell labels and not numbers. Write the formula for cell D9 here. _____ Check this answer with the one listed in the back of the book on page 90.

6. In cell D15, use cell labels to build a formula that computes the grand total. Write the formula that you will type here. _____ Check this with the one listed on page 90.

7. In cell D16, type the formula that will calculate the amount beyond the allocated $60.00 that needs to be contributed to the party fund. Hint: This formula uses a number and a cell location. Write the formula here. _____ Compare it to the formula given in the back of the book.

8. The Finishing Touches

   A. Insert a footer. Type *Activity 9* and <Enter>. Then type *your name* and <Enter>.

   B. Save this spreadsheet to your disk. Name this file *SS Act 9*.

9. Print this spreadsheet, landscape, with the answers showing. Then print the spreadsheet, landscape, with the formulas showing. An alternative to the process that you've been using to show the formulas is to press <CTRL> and the tilde key.

Activity 9: Time to Review and Extend

Answer the following question and adjust your spreadsheet file as indicated. Check your response to the questions with those on page 90, and compare your new spreadsheet files with those on the CD-ROM.

1. What adjustments could you make to the spreadsheet to make the party less expensive? _____

   _____

2. Manipulate the spreadsheet so that the total cost of the party is as close to $60.00 (excluding tax) as you can get without going over. Go to **FILE** and select **Save As**. Name this file *SS Act 9a*.

3. Manipulate the spreadsheet to show what you would purchase if you had a $100.00 budget. See how close you can get without going over the budget. Go to **FILE** and select **Save As**. Name this file *SS Act 9b*.

4. Manipulate the spreadsheet to show what you would purchase if you decided to invite 16 people to the party and you had a $90.00 budget. Go to **FILE** and select **Save As**. Name this file *SS Act 9c*.

5. Why is a spreadsheet a useful tool in planning an event that has a specific budget? _____

   _____

Activity 10: Million Dollars

<u>Overview</u>: You have a million dollars to spend in this activity. You will use a spreadsheet to help you decide how to spend the money.

1. Open a new spreadsheet file.

2. Wow! You have just inherited $1,000,000. Let's see if you can spend <u>exactly</u> one million dollars on 10 different items. You may purchase more than one of each item. Set up your spreadsheet file so that it looks like this.

	A	B	C	D
1	Item	Cost of Item	How Many?	Total
2				
3				
4				
5				
6				
7				
8				
9				
10				
11				
12			Grand Total	

3. Formatting
   A. Right-align the contents of columns B, C, and D.
   B. Format the numbers in columns B and D for Currency.
   C. Add cell color, text color, and borders to the document to make it look visually appealing.

4. In cells A2 through A11, type in the name of each item you would buy if you had a million dollars. After typing all of the information, make column A wide enough to display the longest entry. Your spreadsheet entries should look something like this, based on your purchase choices.

	A	B	C	D
1	Item	Cost of Item	How Many?	Total
2	House			
3	Car			
4	Furnishings			

5. Estimate the cost of each item and type these amounts into cells B2 through B11. After typing the cost of each item, one or more of your cells might be filled with number signs instead of actual numbers.

	A	B
1	Item	Cost of Item
2	House	#######
3	Car	$30,000.00
4	Furnishings	$40,000.00

The pound (or number) symbols indicate that the column is too narrow to display the entire number. Increase the column width by positioning the cursor on the vertical line between column B and column C. Click and drag right until the column is wide enough to display the entire number.

	A	B
1	**Item**	**Cost of Item**
2	House	$ 350,000.00
3	Car	$ 30,000.00
4	Furnishings	$ 40,000.00

6. In column C, type the quantity of each item that you would purchase.

7. In column D, figure out the total cost of each item. Use cell locations to build the formulas. Write the formula that you typed in cell D4 here _____ . Compare this to the formula in the back of the book.

8. Click cell D12. Figure out the Grand Total of all of your purchases. Use cell locations to build this formula. What formula will you type? _____ Compare this with the formula listed in the back of the book. Remember, the Grand Total must add up to exactly $1,000,000. If it does not add up to exactly $1,000,000, then begin experimenting with the numbers. Maybe you need more or less of something. Maybe the cost of an item is too much or too little.

9. Finishing
    A. Insert a footer. Type *Activity 10* and <Enter>. Then type *your name* and <Enter>.
    B. Save the spreadsheet to your disk. Name this file *SS Act 10*.
    C. Print the spreadsheet, landscape, with the answers showing.
    D. Print this spreadsheet, landscape, with the formulas showing. Make sure all parts of the formulas are visible.
    F. Go to **FILE** and select *Exit*.

Activity 10: Time to Review

Why was it so important to use cell locations in the formulas you created in this spreadsheet? _____

Activity 11: Order of Operations

<u>Overview</u>: This activity is designed to familiarize you with the Order of Operations. Specifically, it gives you the opportunity to have the spreadsheet solve several mathematical expressions involving parentheses, powers, and the four standard mathematical operations of addition, subtraction, multiplication, and division.

1. Open a new spreadsheet file.

2. Adding the Data
   A. Type the following entries into the spreadsheet file.

	A	B	C	D	E
1	8	6	4	2	
2					

   B. Select cells A1 through D1.

	A	B	C	D
1	8	6	4	2
2				

   C. Position the cursor so it is located in the lower-right corner of D1. It will become a thin cross. Drag to cell D8 and release the mouse. This should fill the contents of the first row into rows 1 through 8.

	A	B	C	D
1	8	6	4	2
2	8	6	4	2
3	8	6	4	2
4	8	6	4	2
5	8	6	4	2
6	8	6	4	2
7	8	6	4	2
8	8	6	4	2
9				

   D. Add a left border to column E.

	A	B	C	D	E
1	8	6	4	2	
2	8	6	4	2	

3. About the Order of Operations
   The spreadsheet applies the Order of Operations to solve math problems. Calculations are performed in this order:
   A. ( ) Parentheses (hold <Shift> while typing 9 or 0 to get the parentheses)
   B. ^ Powers (hold <Shift> while typing 6); $3 \wedge 2$ is the same as 3^2
   C. *, / Multiplication and Division, from left to right
   D. +, - Addition and Subtraction, from left to right

   • Within parentheses, powers are calculated first, followed by multiplication and division from left to right and then finally addition and subtraction from left to right.
   • If there are computations in the numerator and/or denominator of a fraction, the fraction bar is used to group things. The Order of Operations will be used to compute the numerator, then to compute the denominator. After the numerator and denominator are calculated, the final division is performed.

Activity 11: Order of Operations *(cont.)*

4. Exploring the Order of Operations

A. Problem 1
   Take out a pencil and a piece of paper.
   Apply the Order of Operations as you calculate 8 + 6 * 4 / 2
   What answer did you get? _____
   In what order did you perform the calculations?_____
   Click cell E1 and type *=A1+B1*C1/D1*.
   What answer did the computer display? _____
   Did your answer match the computer's answer? _____ (It should!)

B. Problem 2
   On your paper, apply the Order of Operations to calculate the answer to (8 + 6) * (4 / 2).
   What answer did you get? _____
   In what order did you perform the calculations?_____
   Click cell E2 and type *=(A2+B2)*(C2/D2)*.
   What answer did the computer display? _____
   Did your answer match the computer's answer? _____

C. Problem 3
   On your paper, apply the Order of Operations to calculate the answer to 8 - 6 + 4 ^ 2.
   What answer did you get? _____
   In what order did you perform the calculations?_____
   Click cell E3 and type *=A3-B3+C3^D3*.
   What answer did the computer display? _____
   Did your answer match the computer's answer? _____

D. Problem 4
   On your paper, apply the Order of Operations to calculate the answer to (8 - 6)^(4 / 2).
   What answer did you get? _____
   In what order did you perform the calculations?_____
   Click cell E4 and type *=(A4-B4)^(C4/D4)*.
   What answer did the computer display? _____
   Did your answer match the computer's answer? _____

E. Problem 5
   On your paper, apply the Order of Operations to calculate the answer to 8 * 6 / 4 + 2.
   What answer did you get? _____
   In what order did you perform the calculations?_____
   Click cell E5 and type *=A5*B5/C5+D5*.
   What answer did the computer display? _____
   Did your answer match the computer's answer? _____

Activity 11: Order of Operations *(cont.)*

5. Do You Understand?

    Add (), ^, +, -, *, and / to the contents of cells E6 and E7 respectively to find expressions that equal 2. The order of the cells has to stay the same as with each of the problems in rows 1 through 5; however, the operations can change. Check the answers in the back of the book or on the CD-ROM after you have completed the exercise.

6. A Challenge

    Write down an even number other than 2 here. _____
    In E8, your challenge is to develop an expression that equals the number you wrote above. Good luck!

7. Finishing

    A. In the footer, type *Activity 11*, press <Enter>, and type *your name*.
    B. Save the spreadsheet to your disk. Name the file *SS Act 11*.
    C. Print the spreadsheet with the answers displayed and with the formulas displayed.
    D. Go to **FILE** and select *Exit*.

Activity 11: Time to Review

Answer the following questions. Check your responses with those on page 91.

1. Without looking, see if you can remember the order in which the four levels of computations are performed. Write what you think here.

    _____

    _____

2. Why is Order of Operations important? _____

    _____

Activity 12: PTA 1

Overview: In Activity 12, you will apply the Order of Operations. The context is a PTA fundraiser. You will create several formulas to calculate the cost of the event as well as to compute the profits of the event.

1. Open a new spreadsheet file.

2. Pleasantville Middle School has 500 students. The PTA of this school just held a spaghetti dinner as a fundraiser. The goal was to raise $1000 to purchase additional software for the school's computer lab.
   Let's find out if the PTA reached its goal. Set up the spreadsheet exactly as you see it below. You will need to increase the width of column A. If you need to change the width of additional columns, adjust accordingly.

	A	B
1	Fundraiser: Spaghetti Dinner	
2		
3	Price: Adult Ticket	3
4	Price: Child Ticket	2
5	Adult Tickets: Number Sold	100
6	Child Tickets: Number Sold	100
7	Cost: To Make One Dinner	0.55
8		
9	Cost: To Make All Dinners	
10	Money Made from Ticket Sales	
11	PROFIT	

3. Format the numbers in cells B3, B4, B7, B9, B10, B11 for Currency.

4. Click cell B9. In this cell, you need to type the formula that will compute the cost of making all of the dinners. Use cell locations and Order of Operations to build the formula.
   Hints:
   * Figure out how many people attended this event.
   * Decide how you will use this number to compute the cost of one dinner.
   * What formula will you type in this cell? _____
   Check this answer with the one listed in the back of this book. Then type the formula and press <Enter>.

5. Click cell B10. In this cell, you will type the formula that will compute the total income derived from ticket sales. Use cell locations and Order of Operations to build the formula.
   Hints:
   * Figure out how much money the PTA made from the adult ticket sales.
   * Figure out how much money the PTA made from the children ticket sales.
   * Decide how you will use this information to compute the ticket sale income.
   What formula will you type in this cell? _____ Check this answer with the one listed in the back of this book. Then type the formula and press <Enter>.

Activity 12: PTA 1 *(cont.)*

6. Click cell B11. In this cell, you will calculate the total profit for the event. You will use cell locations to build the formula.
   What formula will you type to perform this calculation? _____
   Check this answer with the one listed in the back of this book. Then type the formula and press <Enter>.

7. Finishing
   A. In the footer, type *Activity 12*, press <Enter>, and type *your name*.
   B. Save the spreadsheet to your disk. Name the file *SS Act 12*.
   C. Print the spreadsheet with answers displayed.
   D. Print the spreadsheet with formulas displayed.
   E. Go to **FILE** and select *Exit*.

Activity 12: Time to Review and Extend

Answer the following question and adjust your spreadsheet file as indicated. Check your response to the question with that on page 91.

1. If you increase the adult ticket price by $2.00, you will sell only 90 adult tickets and 90 children's tickets. Type this information into the spreadsheet. What is the new profit? _____

2. In column C, add numbers to reflect the ticket price, number of tickets sold, and the cost per meal that you believe would be realistic for a PTA fundraiser in your area. Click cell B9. Position the cursor in the lower-right corner of the cell and Fill Right. Do the same thing in cells B10 and B11. How does your profit compare to the original profit listed in the spreadsheet (before the change in problem 1 above)? _____

_____

Activity 13: PTA 2

Overview: In Activity 12, the PTA did not reach its goal of a $1,000 profit. Members wonder where they went wrong and what changes they should make so that next year's spaghetti dinner fundraiser will generate a higher profit. Adjust the spreadsheet from Activity 12 to see how various changes influence overall profits. If you did not complete Activity 12, you can access the template on the CD.

1. Open the file called *SS Act 12*.
   A. <u>If you completed SS Act 12</u>: Find the file called *SS Act 12* on your floppy disk or hard drive. Double-click this file to open it.
   <u>If you did not complete SS Act 12</u>: Insert the book's CD-ROM from into the computer. Double-click **My Computer** from the desktop. Double-click the CD-ROM icon. Find the file called *SS Act 12* and double-click to open.
   B. Make sure the spreadsheet's formulas are NOT displayed. If you see the formulas, press <CTRL> and the tilde key.

2. Go to **FILE**, choose *Page Setup*, and click on the **Landscape** option.

3. Go to **FILE** and select *Save As*. Name the file *SS Act 13*.

4. Select cells B9 through B11.

	A	B	C	D
1	Fundraiser: Spaghetti Dinner			
2				
3	Price: Adult Ticket	$ 3.00		
4	Price: Child Ticket	$ 2.00		
5	Adult Tickets: Number Sold	100		
6	Child Tickets: Number Sold	100		
7	Cost: To Make One Dinner	$ 0.55		
8				
9	Cost: To Make All Dinners	$ 110.00		
10	Money Made from Ticket Sales	$ 500.00		
11	PROFIT	$ 390.00		

5. Fill the formulas to the right up through column F. Since there are no contents in C3 through F7, some of the included cells will remain empty.

6. Experiment with the numbers in columns C, D, E, and F until you reach the profit goal of exactly $1000. Change whatever numbers you want to change as long as the changes are reasonable and your profit is exactly $1000.

   Possibilities to consider: What if more people come to this event? Remember, 500 students attend this school. What if the dinner was less expensive to make? What if the tickets cost more? What if the tickets cost less?

7. Finishing
   A. In the footer, type *Activity 13*, press <Enter>, and type *your name*.
   B. Go to **FILE** and select *Save*. Name the file *SS Act 13*.
   C. Print the spreadsheet with answers displayed.
   D. Print the spreadsheet with formulas displayed.
   E. Go to **FILE** and select *Exit*.

Activity 13: Time to Review

Examine the information that you typed into the spreadsheet columns to get the goal of a $1,000 profit. If you were asked by the PTA how to increase profits for next year, how would you respond? Put your ideas into words below. Justify your position.

_____

_____

_____

_____

Activity 14: Favorite Treat Column Chart

<u>Overview</u>: Activity 14 teaches you how to create a column chart in *Microsoft Excel*. In this case, the data comes from a survey of student food preferences. However, what you learn about column charts can be applied to any information.

1. Open a new spreadsheet file.

2. Mrs. Brown recently surveyed the students in her computer classes. She asked them several questions. One question was, "What is your favorite after school treat?" Their choices included candy, chips, cookies or pizza.

   To graph the results, set up a spreadsheet file so it looks exactly like this.

	A	B
1	**Favorite Treats**	**Number of Votes**
2	Candy	18
3	Chips	40
4	Cookies	80
5	Pizza	12

3. Widen any columns that need to be widened.

4. Center-align the contents of cell B1.

5. Creating the Column Chart
   You use a Column Chart when you want to compare numerical quantities.
   A. Select cells A1 through B5.

	A	B
1	**Favorite Treats**	**Number of Votes**
2	Candy	18
3	Chips	40
4	Cookies	80
5	Pizza	12

   B. Click the **Chart Wizard** button from the Standard Toolbar.

   The **Chart Wizard** will take you through 4 steps. After completing the steps, a chart will be produced.

Activity 14: Favorite Treat Column Chart *(cont.)*

C. In Step 1 of the **Chart Wizard**, click **Column** and choose the **Clustered Column** sub-type. Click **Next**.

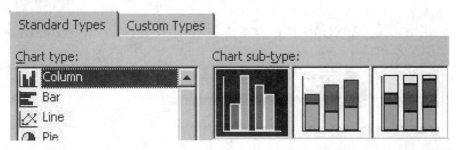

D. In Step 2, you can either choose to select data from rows or columns. The data will be displayed in the chart differently based on your selection. Look at the sample when **Columns** is selected. Then view the sample when **Rows** is selected. Choose the option you prefer.

E. In Step 3, type *Favorite Treats* into the **Chart Title** box. If you wish to type in a label for the x- or y-axis, you can do that as well. Click **Next**.

F. In the last step, Step 4, select "As object in Sheet 1." Click **Finish**.
Your chart should look similar to this if you chose the **Rows** option in Step 2. If you chose **Columns**, it will look a little different.

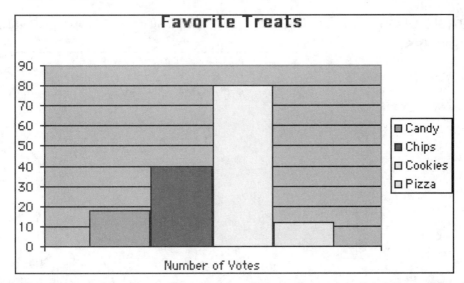

G. Click in the white area of the chart and drag the entire object beneath cell A5. To erase the chart, click on it to select it, and then press <Backspace>.

6. Finishing
A. In the footer, type *Activity 14*, press <Enter>, and type *your name*.
B. Go to **FILE** and select *Save*. Name the file *SS Act 14*.
C. Print the spreadsheet in landscape format.
D. Go to **FILE** and select *Exit*.

Activity 14: Time to Review

Let's find out how much you learned about column charts. Compare your responses to those on page 91.

1. Summarize the data displayed in the chart you created in Activity 14.

   _____

   _____

   _____

2. Complete this sentence: You use a column chart_____

   _____

3. Give an example of data that could be graphed using a column chart in a Social Studies class. _____

   _____

4. Given an example of data that could be graphed using a column chart in a Language Arts class. _____

Activity 15: Getting Fancy with Column Charts

<u>Overview</u>: You will learn more about column charts in this activity, as you graph a comparison of two different data groups. In addition to creating a column chart that depicts the comparison, you will also learn how to change the format of the chart itself. This includes changing labels, gridlines, titles, and legends. It also includes changing the color of the columns.

1. Open a new spreadsheet file.

2. Mrs. Brown recently polled all the students attending Pleasantville Middle School. One of the questions she asked was, "What is your favorite cafeteria lunch?" The choices students could select from included hot dogs, burgers, tacos, pizza or spaghetti. There were some interesting differences when the results were examined by gender.

Favorite Lunch	Boys	Girls
Burgers	60	40
Hot Dogs	70	20
Pizza	60	60
Spaghetti	20	60
Tacos	35	50

   Create a spreadsheet file that includes this information. You should have data in cells A1 to C6.

3. Select the contents of cells A1 through C6 for inclusion in a column chart. Use the **Chart Wizard**, and follow the instructions from Activity 14 if necessary.

4. Chart Customization
   A. After the chart is created, edit it by first clicking once in the white space inside the chart. Then go to **CHART**. Choose **Chart Options**.
   B. Click the **Titles** tab. Add labels for the x- and y-axis if you did not created them initially.
   C. Click the **Gridlines** tab. Get rid of the check in front of **Value (Y) Axis, Major Gridlines**.
   D. Click the **Legend** tab. Change the placement of the legend to **Bottom**.
   E. Click the **Data Labels** tab. Click **Show Values**. Click **OK**.
   F. Click on one of the columns that represents data from boys. This should put a little box in each of the boy columns.

   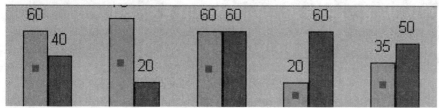

   G. Right-click on one of the columns. Choose **Format Data Series**. In the window that appears, choose a color that you would like to use to represent the boys' data. Then click the **Fill Effects** button.

Activity 15: Getting Fancy with Column Charts *(cont.)*

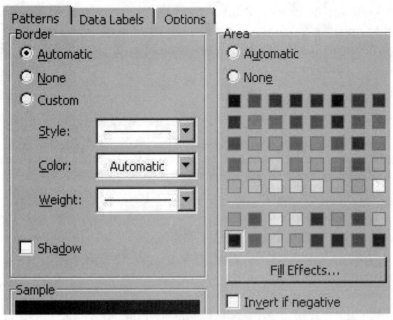

Experiment with the **Gradients**, **Textures**, and **Patterns** tabs until you are satisfied with the outcome.

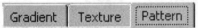

H. Make similar changes to the girls' bars.

I. Your chart should look something like this.

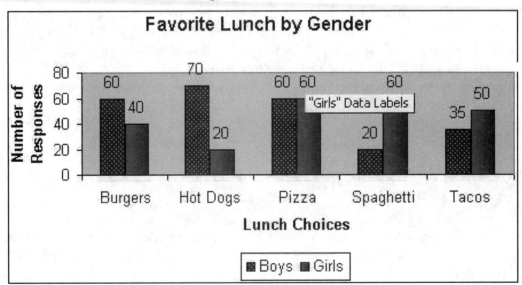

5. Click cell B5 and change the number to *40*. Watch the chart as you press <Enter>. Explain what happened. _____

Activity 15: Getting Fancy with Column Charts *(cont.)*

6. Finishing
    A. In the footer, type *Activity 15*, press <Enter>, and type *your name*.
    B. Go to **FILE** and select *Save*. Name the file *SS Act 15*.
    C. Print the spreadsheet in portrait format.
    D. Go to **FILE** and select *Exit*.

Activity 15: Time to Review and Extend

Answer the following questions. Check your responses with those on page 91.

1. How would you use the information in the chart to decide what food items to order if you were throwing a party? _____

    _____

    _____

2. Why is it useful that the bars automatically adjust if you make a change to the spreadsheet data? _____

    _____

    _____

3. Give an example of how a principal could use a column chart to display data. _____

    _____

    _____

Activity 16: Favorite Sport Bar Chart

<u>Overview</u>: In *Microsoft Excel*, you can create several different chart types. In this activity, you will learn how to create a second type, a bar chart.

1. Open a new spreadsheet file.

2. Mrs. Brown recently surveyed the students in her computer classes. One of the questions she asked was, "What is your favorite sport?" She gave students the following four options from which to select: basketball, football, hockey or volleyball.

   Enter the following results into the spreadsheet file.

	A	B
1	**Favorite Sport**	**Number of Votes**
2	Basketball	50
3	Football	65
4	Hockey	25
5	Volleyball	10

3. Widen the columns that need to be widened, and make any other desired format changes to the spreadsheet, including alignment.

4. Creating a Bar Chart
   You use a bar chart when you want to compare things. This is true for both a column chart, as in Activity 14 and Activity 15, as well as bar charts.
   A. Select cells A1 through B5.
   B. Click the **Chart Wizard** button from the Standard Toolbar.
   C. Choose **Bar** and then select the **Clustered Bar** sub-type. Click **Next**.

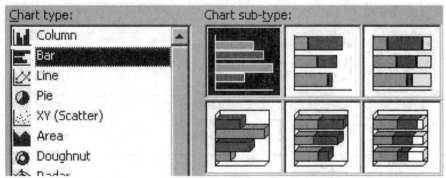

   D. Decide whether you wish to choose data from Rows or Columns. Click **Next** after you make your selection. Click **Next**.
   E. Click on the various tabs in Step 3 to alter labels, gridlines, and format. Once you are satisfied with your selections, click **Next**.
   F. Keep the chart as an object in Sheet 1. Click **Finish**.

Activity 16: Favorite Sport Bar Chart *(cont.)*

G. Your chart should look something like this.

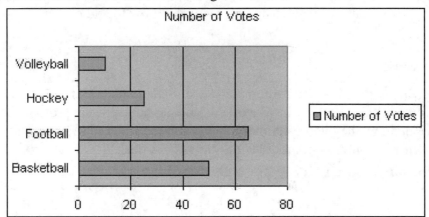

H. Click somewhere on the white area of the chart and drag the whole chart below cell A5.

5. Finishing
   A. In the footer, type *Activity 16*, press <Enter>, and type *your name*.
   B. Go to **FILE** and select *Save*. Name the file *SS Act 16*.
   C. Print the spreadsheet in portrait format.
   D. Go to **FILE** and select *Exit*.

Activity 17: Getting Fancy with Bar Charts

<u>Overview</u>: This activity extends and expands the skills introduced in Activity 16. You will learn to create bar charts that compare two groups of data. You will also learn how to add clip art to the spreadsheet.

1. Open a new spreadsheet file.

2. Annie and Billy are brother and sister. Each summer, they run a lemonade stand on the corner of the street where they live. In the past, they have worked together and split the profits. This year, however, they have decided that they will each individually run the stand for a week and keep their own profits. Organize the information below into the spreadsheet.

Lemonade Stand	Annie's Profits	Billy's Profits
Monday	15	20
Tuesday	20	15
Wednesday	30	25
Thursday	3	10
Friday	7.5	10

3. Format the numbers in columns B and C to be displayed as Currency.

4. Put a bottom border below cells B6 and C6.

5. Click cell B7. Use the SUM function to compute Annie's total profit for the week. Do the same thing in C7 for Billy.

6. Use the information in your spreadsheet to create a bar chart. If needed, review pages 50-51. When you select the data for the chart, DO NOT select the information in cells B7 and C7. You might need to move the chart and/or resize it. Your chart should look like this.

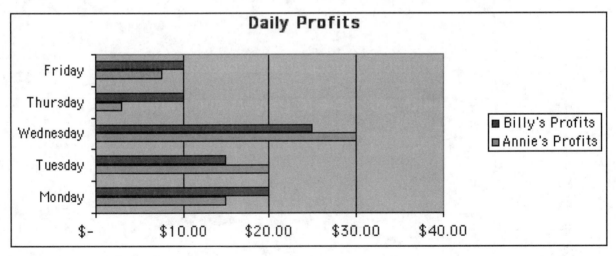

Activity 17: Getting Fancy with Bar Charts *(cont.)*

7. Adding Clip Art

A. Go to **INSERT** and select *Picture*, *Clip Art*.

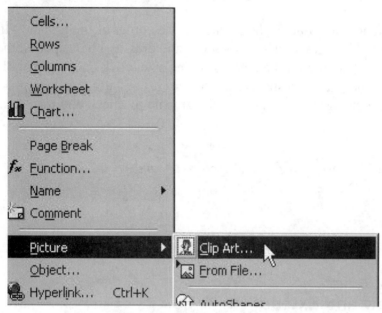

B. A Clip Art window will appear. Choose the category of Clip Art that contains an image you would like to insert, or type a word to search for in the search box.

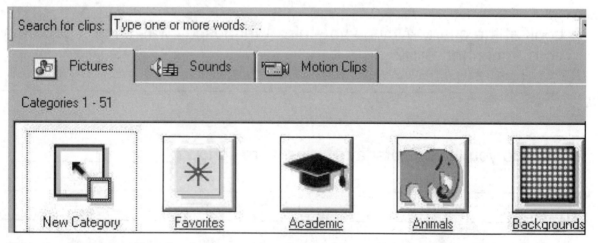

C. Once you find a graphic that is acceptable, click it. Then click the **Insert Clip** button from the selection that appears.

Activity 17: Getting Fancy with Bar Charts *(cont.)*

   D. After clicking this button, you can return to your spreadsheet by either clicking the **X** in the upper-right corner of the Clip Art window, or you can click **Microsoft Excel** in the Task Bar across the bottom of your screen.

   E. To resize the graphic, click and drag one of the squares in the corner of the graphic. If you want to move the whole graphic, click in the middle of it and drag to a new spot on the spreadsheet. Once you are satisfied with the placement and size, click once outside of the graphic. The image can be moved and resized many times. If you later decide to make additional size or placement changes, click once on the graphic to select, and then resize or move.

8. Finishing
   A. In the footer, type *Activity 17*, press \<Enter\>, and type *your name*.
   B. Go to **FILE** and select *Save*. Name the file *SS Act 17*.
   C. Print the spreadsheet in portrait format.
   D. Go to **FILE** and select *Exit*.

Activity 17: Time to Review and Extend

Answer the following questions. Check your responses with those on page 92.

1. Look at the chart. Why do you think Wednesday was such a good day for both Annie and Billy? _____

   _____

   _____

2. Why do you think Thursday's sales were so low? _____

   _____

   _____

3. When you examine the data in bar chart form, does it appear that either Annie or Billy has a much higher profit than the other?

   _____

4. According to data in row 7 of your spreadsheet, does one of the children have a higher profit than the other one? _____

   _____

   _____

Activity 18: Sleepy Pie Chart

<u>Overview</u>: The focus of this activity is creating pie charts. You will develop a spreadsheet file from which data will be displayed in a pie chart format.

1. Open a new spreadsheet file.

2. Mrs. Brown recently polled all the students attending Pleasantville Middle School. One of the questions she asked was, "Do you get enough sleep each night?"
   Enter the following information, which represents the responses.
   Enough Sleep?
   Yes   175
   No   325

3. Pie Chart
   You use a Pie Chart when you want to make comparisons based on parts of the whole.
   A. Select the spreadsheet data.
   B. Click the **Chart Wizard** button.
   C. Choose **Pie** as the chart option and choose either the **Pie** or **Pie with a 3D visual effect** sub-type.
   D. You should not need to make any changes in Step 2; the data series should come from columns.
   E. In Step 3 of the **Chart Wizard**, add a title, and make any other changes you wish to make to the format of the chart.
   F. After finishing the last step, your chart should look something like this.

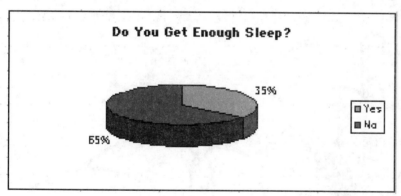

4. Finishing
   A. In the footer, type *Activity 18*, press <Enter>, and type *your name*.
   B. Go to **FILE** and select *Save*. Name the file *SS Act 18*.
   C. Print the spreadsheet in portrait format.
   D. Go to **FILE** and select *Exit*.

Activity 18: Time to Review and Extend

Answer the following questions. Check your responses with those on page 92.

1. Study the chart you created. What recommendations could you make to parents based on this data? _____

   _____

2. Study the chart you created. What recommendations could you make to the superintendent based on this data? _____

   _____

3. Give an example in which you could use a pie chart in a Math class to display data. _____

   _____

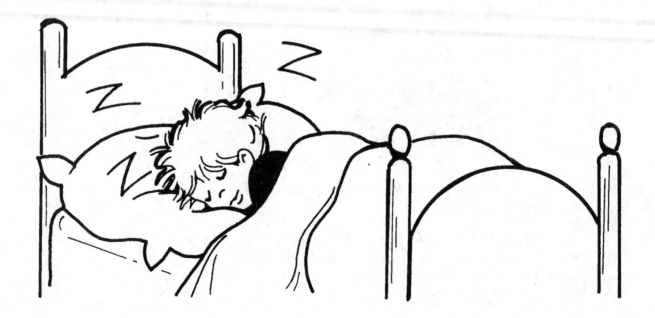

Activity 19: Getting Fancy with Pie Charts

Overview: As in Activity 18, you will create a spreadsheet and corresponding pie chart with format changes. You will also learn how to sort information within a spreadsheet program.

1. Open a new spreadsheet file.

2. Mrs. Brown recently surveyed the 30 students in her first hour computer class. She asked students, "What color eyes do you have?" Type these responses into a spreadsheet file.

	A	B
1		**Responses**
2	Blue	8
3	Brown	17
4	Gray	3
5	Green	2

3. Widen any columns that need to be widened.

4. Center-align the contents of column B.

5. Sorting the Spreadsheet Data
   Spreadsheet programs allow you to sort data alphabetically and numerically. When sorting spreadsheet data, it is crucial to select all of the information that is associated with the data to be sorted. Otherwise, while some of the data may be rearranged, other data will stay in its original location. This is problematic.

   A. Click and drag to select cells A2 through B5. Do not include cells A1 and B1 in the group of selected cells because there is no need to sort labels.

	A	B
1		**Responses**
2	Blue	8
3	Brown	17
4	Gray	3
5	Green	2

   B. Go to **DATA** and select *Sort*.

   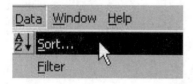

   C. A Sort Window appears. In this window, you will make several changes to the default values.

   The data had been listed alphabetically by eye color at first. We want to sort numerically now based on eye color. In the **Sort by** window, select column B. You can designate whether you want the data arranged lowest to highest (ascending) or highest to lowest (descending). At the bottom of the window, put a dot in the circle that indicates there is no header row.

Activity 19: Getting Fancy with Pie Charts *(cont.)*

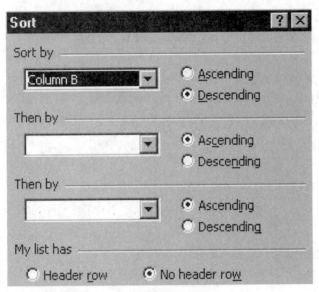

D. Your data should now look like this.

	A	B
1		**Responses**
2	Brown	17
3	Blue	8
4	Gray	3
5	Green	2

You should note that the number of students with each eye color is the same in both versions of the spreadsheet. Only the order in which they are listed has changed.

6. Pie Chart
   A. Select cells A1 through B5.
   B. Click the **Chart Wizard** in the Standard Bar.
   C. Choose **Pie** as the chart option.
   D. Add the percents to the data labels.
   E. Your chart should look like this.

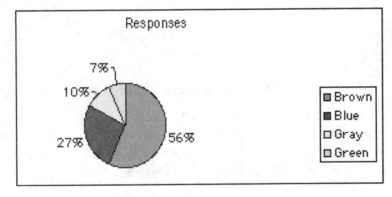

Activity 19: Getting Fancy with Pie Charts *(cont.)*

7. Finishing
   A. In the footer, type *Activity 19*, press <Enter>, and type *your name*.
   B. Go to **FILE** and select *Save*. Name the file *SS Act 19*.
   C. Print the spreadsheet in portrait format.
   D. Go to **FILE** and select *Exit*.

Activity 19: Time to Review and Extend

Answer the following questions. Check your responses with those on page 92.

1. Complete this sentence: You use a pie chart to _____

   _____

2. Give an example of how the Student Council could use a pie chart to display data. _____

   _____

3. What would happen if you performed a sort after selecting just the following data?

	A	B
1		Responses
2	Blue	8
3	Brown	17
4	Gray	3
5	Green	2

   _____

   _____

Activity 20: Line Chart–Bowling Scores

Overview: In this activity, you will learn how to create line graphs in *Microsoft Excel*.

1. Open a new spreadsheet file.

2. Billy is 14 years old and he is interested in becoming a good bowler. In fact, his goal is to be one of the best bowlers in the Student Bowling League. Let's take a look at his average scores for the last six months to see how he is doing.

   Set up a spreadsheet file so that it contains the following information.

	A	B
1	January	200
2	February	175
3	March	200
4	April	225
5	May	250
6	June	250

3. Line Chart
   You use a line chart when you want to see how values have changed over a period of time. A line chart makes it easy to identify a trend, if one exists.
   A. Select cells A1 through B6.
   B. Click the **Chart Wizard** button from the Standard Toolbar.
   C. Choose **Line** and select the sub-type you desire.
   D. In Step 3, click the **Title** tab and type *Billy's Bowling Average* as the chart title. Then click the **Legend** tab and remove the check in front of "Show Legend."
   E. In the **Labels** menu, get rid of the check next to "Legend."
      Your chart should look like this.

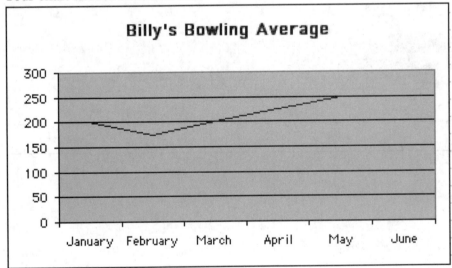

4. Finishing
   A. In the footer, type *Activity 20*, press <Enter>, and type *your name*.
   B. Go to **FILE** and select *Save*. Name the file *SS Act 20*.
   C. Print the spreadsheet in landscape format.
   D. Go to **FILE** and select *Exit*.

Activity 20: Time to Review and Extend

Answer the following questions. Check your responses with those on page 92.

1. Summarize the data displayed in this chart. Describe the trend.

   _____

   _____

   _____

2. What do you think Billy's bowling score will be for the month of July? Why do you believe this will be his average that month?

   _____

   _____

   _____

3. Describe when a line chart would be an appropriate chart to use. _____

   _____

4. Give an example in which you could use a line chart in a Math class to display data._____

   _____

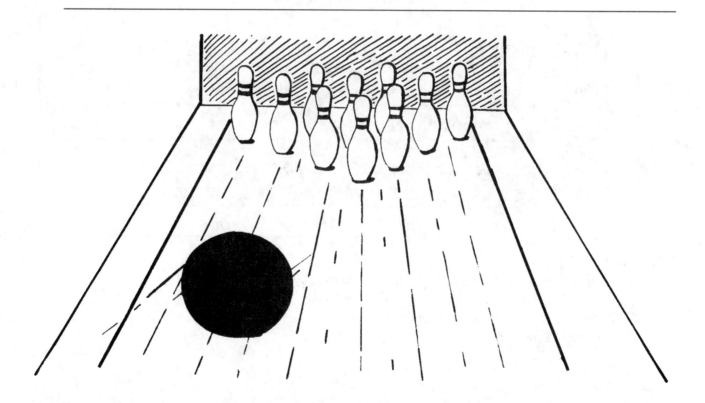

Activity 21: Line Chart Comparison of Two Data Sets

<u>Overview</u>: You will use a line chart to compare profits during the same quarters in two different school years.

1. Open a new spreadsheet file.

2. It's June and the manager of the school store at Pleasantville Middle School is getting ready to order supplies for next September. The manager wants to examine trends over the past two years before making any ordering decisions. Type the following information into the spreadsheet file.

	A	B	C
1		2000 Profit	2001 Profit
2	Term 1	$ 750.00	$ 950.00
3	Term 2	$ 450.00	$ 500.00
4	Term 3	$ 450.00	$ 450.00
5	Term 4	$ 200.00	$ 200.00

3. Format Changes
   A. Widen the columns that need to be widened.
   B. Center the contents of columns B and C.
   C. Format the numbers in columns B and C to be displayed as currency.

4. Create a Line Chart
   Select the contents of cells A1 through C5. If you need to review the steps in creating a line chart, see pages 60-61.
   Your chart should look like this.

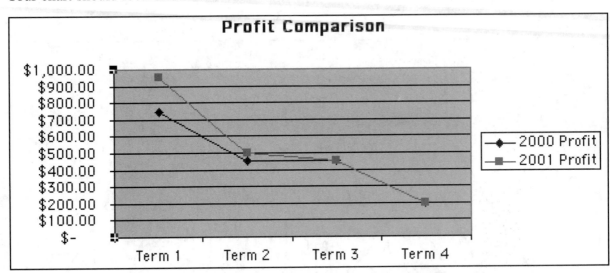

5. Finishing
   A. In the footer, type *Activity 21*, press <Enter>, and type *your name*.
   B. Go to **FILE** and select *Save*. Name the file *SS Act 21*.
   C. Print the spreadsheet in landscape format.
   D. Go to **FILE** and select *Exit*.

Activity 21: Time to Review and Extend

Answer the following questions. Check your responses with those on page 92.

1. Summarize the data displayed in this chart. Describe the trend.

   _____

   _____

2. How will the information displayed in this chart help the store manager to
   order supplies for September?_____

   _____

   _____

3. Give an example in which you could use a line chart in a Science class to
   display a comparison of two (or more) similar types of data.

   _____

   _____

Activity 22: Average It!

<u>Overview</u>: You will learn about the AVERAGE function. After learning about the function, you will use this function in a spreadsheet to calculate the average of sets of numbers.

1. Open a new spreadsheet file.

2. Set up the spreadsheet file so it looks like this.

	A	B	C	D	E
1		23	1998		
2		45	3456		
3		67	2134		
4		89	5678		
5		23	3214		
6		45	8765		
7		12	9876		
8		35	2334		
9		67	1212		
10		82	5957		
11					
12	Average				

3. Change column widths as needed.

4. About the AVERAGE Function.
A spreadsheet program has a number of defined formulas called functions. These are calculations that the spreadsheet knows how to compute. We worked with the SUM function in Activity 3. The AVERAGE function is another one of these defined formulas.

What does the AVERAGE function do?
The AVERAGE function automatically calculates the average or mean of the numbers found in a range of cells. The cells can be located within columns or rows.
What does the AVERAGE function look like?

As you recall from earlier activities, all formulas begin with an equal sign. This applies to the AVERAGE function. A range of cells to which the function will be applied must be specified. An example is =AVERAGE(A1:A10). The word "Average" is <u>not</u> case sensitive.
How does the AVERAGE function work?

To use the AVERAGE function to determine the mean of the numbers located in cells A2, B2, C2, D2, E2, F2 and G2, you first click the cell in which you would like the average to be displayed. Next, type =AVERAGE(A2:G2) into the selected cell. Press <Enter>. The average will then be automatically calculated and displayed in this cell.

5. Click cell B12. Type =AVERAGE(B1:B10). Press <Enter>.
What happened?_____

6. More Averages
    A. Click cell B12.
    B. Position the mouse in the lower-right corner of that cell (it becomes a thin cross).
    C. Drag to cell E12. The function will fill right.
    D. Since data has not yet been added to columns D and E, D12 and E12 remain temporarily empty.
    E. If you see the pound (or number) symbols in any of the cells, that means the column is not wide enough to display the number. If necessary, increase the column width.

7. Add data to columns D and E. As you enter the numbers, watch what happens to the displayed average in row 12.

8. Format the numbers in cells B12, C12, D12, and E12 so no decimals are displayed. Click once on the **Decrease Decimal** button from the Formatting Toolbar.

9. Finishing
    A. In the footer, type *Activity 22*, press <Enter>, and type *your name*.
    B. Go to **FILE** and select *Save*. Name the file *SS Act 22*.
    C. Print the spreadsheet in portrait format with the answers showing.
    D. Then print the spreadsheet in portrait format with the formulas showing.
    E. Go to **FILE** and select *Exit*.

Activity 22: Time to Review and Extend

Answer the following questions. Check your responses with those on page 92.

1. If you wanted to find the average of numbers in cells C3 through Y3 in a spreadsheet, what would the function look like? _____

2. Describe how the AVERAGE function works. _____

    _____

3. What is the formula that you could use (instead of using the AVERAGE function) that would compute the average of the numbers in cells B1 through B10?_____

4. What is the advantage of using the AVERAGE function over using this formula? _____

    _____

Activity 23: Grades

Overview: This spreadsheet activity uses the AVERAGE function to compute student grades. You will also learn how to hide columns so that you can graph data in non-adjacent columns.

1. Open a new spreadsheet file.

2. Set up your spreadsheet file like this.

	A	B	C	D	E	F
1	**Math 5th Hour**	Test 1	Test 2	Test 3	Test 4	Final Grade
2	Artley, Mike	80	85	90	100	
3	Brennen, Mary	92	93	90	93	
4	Ahmed, Ali	82	85	87	92	
5	Leonard, Leonard	75	82	89	90	
6	Ways, Bill	100	85	90	94	
7	**Class Average**					

3. Right-align the words in cells B1, C1, D1, E1 and F1.

4. Mike Artley's Final Grade
   A. Click cell F2.
   B. Type =AVERAGE(B2:E2). Press <Enter>.

5. Fill the function down to cell F6.

6. Class Average for Test 1
   A. Click cell B7.
   B. Type =AVERAGE(B2:B6). Press <Enter>.

7. Fill the function to the right through cell F7.

8. Create a Chart Using Non-Adjacent Spreadsheet Column Contents
   There are times in which you might want to create a chart that includes information from one column and another column that is not next to it. An example would be a chart of class averages that includes student names, where the names and averages are not in adjacent columns. If the names were positioned in the column adjacent to the averages, then you could select the data in both columns and proceed by clicking the **Chart Wizard** button. When the columns are not adjacent to each other, then an additional step needs to be applied.
   A. Select cells A2 through A6.
   B. Press the <CTRL> key (Command key on a Macintosh) and select cells E2 through E6. The result should look like this.

	A	B	C	D	E	F
1	**Math 5th Hour**	Test 1	Test 2	Test 3	Test 4	Final Grade
2	Artley, Mike	80	85	90	100	88.75
3	Brennen, Mary	92	93	90	93	92
4	Ahmed, Ali	82	85	87	92	86.5
5	Leonard, Leonard	75	82	89	90	84
6	Ways, Bill	100	85	90	94	92.25
7	**Class Average**	85.8	86	89.2	93.8	88.7

By holding the <CTRL> key, you can select as many columns as you wish, regardless of location.

Activity 23: Grades *(cont.)*

C. Now click the **Chart Wizard** button from the Standard Toolbar and decide which type of graph you wish to produce. A pie chart is probably not the best representation. Why?

D. Produce the chart.

E. Resize and move the chart so it does not cover any of the chart data.

9. Finishing

A. In the footer, type *Activity 23*, press <Enter>, and type *your name*.

B. Go to **FILE** and select *Save*. Name the file *SS Act 23*.

C. Print the spreadsheet in portrait format with the answers showing.

D. Then print the spreadsheet in portrait format with the formulas showing.

E. Go to **FILE** and select *Exit*.

Activity 23: Time to Review and Extend

Answer the following questions. Check your responses with those on page 92.

1. Why will the AVERAGE function work to accurately compute student grades in this spreadsheet? _____

_____

2. Why was it necessary to hold the <CTRL> key when selecting data for the chart?

_____

_____

3. Instead of using the <CTRL> key (or Command key on a Macintosh), there is another way to hide columns. Complete the following steps using *SS Act 23*.

A. Select cells A1 through F6.

	A	B	C	D	E	F
1	Math 5th Hour	Test 1	Test 2	Test 3	Test 4	Final Grade
2	Artley, Mike	80	85	90	100	88.75
3	Brennen, Mary	92	93	90	93	92
4	Ahmed, Ali	82	85	87	92	86.5
5	Leonard, Leonard	75	82	89	90	84
6	Ways, Bill	100	85	90	94	92.25
7	Class Average	85.8	86	89.2	93.8	88.7

B. Go to **EDIT** and select *Copy*.

C. Click the **Sheet 2** tab near the bottom of the screen.

Sheet1 \ **Sheet2** / Sheet3

Activity 23: Time to Review and Extend *(cont.)*

D. Click cell A1.

E. Go to **EDIT** and select *Paste*. After the cell contents are pasted, you may need to adjust column width.

F. Click column labels B through E.

	A	B	C	D	E	F
1	Math 5th Hour	Test 1	Test 2	Test 3	Test 4	Final Grade
2	Artley, Mike	80	85	90	100	88.75
3	Brennen, Mary	92	93	90	93	92
4	Ahmed, Ali	82	85	87	92	86.5
5	Leonard, Leonard	75	82	89	90	84
6	Ways, Bill	100	85	90	94	92.25
7	Class Average	85.8	86	89.2	93.8	88.7

G. Go to **FORMAT** and choose *Column*, *Hide*.

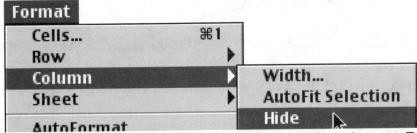

H. Now select A2 through F6. Even though columns B through E are still part of your spreadsheet, they are hidden from view and therefore are not selected.

	A	F
1	Math 5th Hour	Final Grade
2	Artley, Mike	88.75
3	Brennen, Mary	92

I. Now make a column graph of the data and place it below cell C7.

J. Click column A and drag to column F. This also selects everything in between.

	A	F
1	Math 5th Hour	Final Grade
2	Artley, Mike	88.75
3	Brennen, Mary	92

K. Go to **FORMAT**, select *Column*, *Unhide*.

L. What happened to the graph after unhiding all of the columns? _____

_____

M. Why is it better to use <CTRL> (Command on a Macintosh) instead of the Hide option when selecting non-adjacent columns?_____

_____

N. Save the file. This file now contains Sheet 1 and Sheet 2.

Activity 24: Grades–Differing Point Values

Overview: In Activity 23, the AVERAGE function was used to compute grades because all of the assessments were worth 100 points. When tests and assignments are worth varying amounts, you need to use a combination of functions and formulas to calculate grades. In this activity, you will alter the spreadsheet file that was created in Activity 23 so that grades can be calculated even when assignment values do not all equal 100 points. The use of dollar signs within a function will be introduced as well.

1. Open *SS Act 23*. If you completed the activity, open the saved file from your disk or hard drive. If you did not complete the activity, open the file from the CD-ROM.

2. Click the graph to select it. Then go to **EDIT**, select *Clear*, and choose *All*.

3. Go to **FILE** and select *Save As*. Name the file *SS Act 24*.

4. Select cells F2 through F7. Go to **EDIT**, select *Clear*, and choose *Contents*. This will delete the contents of those cells.

5. Select row 2. Then go to **INSERT** and choose *Rows*. This will add an empty row above Mike's scores. Possible points for each assignment will be displayed in this row. Type *100* for Test 1 and Test 3, and type *50* for Test 2 and Test 4.

6. Adjust the borders so that there is a bottom border below the possible points on each test.

7. Change the student data for Test 2 and Test 4 to reflect scores out of 50 instead of 100. Your numbers should match the numbers below.

	A	B	C	D	E	F
1	Math 5th Hour	Test 1	Test 2	Test 3	Test 4	Final Grade
2		100	50	100	50	
3	Artley, Mike	80	45	90	47	
4	Brennen, Mary	92	43	90	42	
5	Ahmed, Ali	82	48	87	39	
6	Leonard, Leonard	75	38	89	40	
7	Ways, Bill	100	41	90	46	
8	Class Average	85.8	43	89.2	42.8	

8. If we took the average of each student's scores at this point, the result would not accurately represent each person's grade. Instead, we will need to calculate each students' total points and compare that total to the total number of points possible.
   A. Click F2.
   B. Type *=SUM(B2:E2)*. Click <Enter>.
   C. Fill this function down to cell F7.

Activity 24: Grades–Different Point Values *(cont.)*

9. Calculating Grades
   A. Which cell contains Mike's total points? _____
   B. Which cell contains the total possible points? _____
   C. To compute Mike's percent, what formula should be typed?_____
      Compare this to the answer on page 93.
   D. Click cell G3.
   E. Type the formula that you wrote in step C after checking its accuracy.
   F. Fill this formula down to the other cells in column G.
   G. With the cells selected, click the **Percent** button in the Formatting Toolbar.

   %

10. One Adjustment (Dollar Signs)
   A. It is likely that there are some errors if you examine some of the calculated percentages. Some are over 100%, which should not be the case since no one has earned more than the total possible points. Let's examine the reason for the error and then correct it.
   B. Click cell G3. Write the formula displayed in the Entry Bar here. _____
   C. Does this formula divide the student's total by the total possible?_____
   D. Click cell G4. Write the formula displayed in the Entry Bar here. _____
   E. Does this formula divide the student's total by the total possible?_____
   F. When you performed the Fill Down, the spreadsheet tried to follow the pattern that had been established with the formula used with Mike's data. Since the formula you constructed took the score from one cell and divided that by the number in the cell directly above it, this was the pattern that was pasted to the other cells. It works for Mike's percent, but not for the others. We need to make one minor adjustment to correct the error.
   G. Click cell G3. In the entry bar, change the formula to $=F3/\$F\$2$ and <Enter>. The dollar signs force the spreadsheet to keep the F2 part of the formula constant when performing the Fill Down. In terms of the formula, $\$F\$2$ is still interpreted as F2 when determining the value to use in the calculation.
   H. Fill the formula through cell G7.
   I. Click cell G4. Does this formula divide the student's total by the total possible? _____

11. Make adjustments to the font color, size, etc. as desired.

12. Finishing
   A. In the footer, type *Activity 24*, press <Enter>, and type *your name*.
   B. Go to **FILE** and select *Save*.
   C. Print the spreadsheet in portrait format with the answers showing.
   D. Then print the spreadsheet in landscape format with the formulas showing.
   E. Go to **FILE** and select *Exit*.

Activity 24: Time to Review and Extend

Answer the following questions. Check your responses with those on page 93.

1. Why did you have to use a formula instead of the AVERAGE function to compute grades in this case? _____

   _____

2. What did the dollar signs do in the formula? _____

   _____

3. When should dollar signs be included in formulas? _____

   _____

MARSHALL MIDDLE SCHOOL

STUDENT: Melinda Maury   DATE: 03/28/02
GRADE: 7   SUBJECT: Microsoft Excel

Attendance	100%	A
Homework	95%	A
Tests	95%	A
Projects	100%	A

Thank you for your Good Work ★

INSTRUCTOR: James P. Johnson

Activity 25: Weighted Grades

Overview: In Activity 24, you learned how to use a formula to compute a student's percent. There are times, however, in which performance on certain activities is weighted in terms of how each factors into an overall grade. Activity 25 provides you with the opportunity to develop a spreadsheet in which homework counts for 25% of the grade, quizzes account for 25% of the grade, and tests contribute to 50% of the course grade.

1. Open a new spreadsheet file.

2. Input the following information into the spreadsheet, and format the cells accordingly.

	A	B	C	D	E	F	G	H	I	J	K	L	M	N	O	P	Q
1		HW1	HW2	Q1	T1	HW3	Q2	Q3	T2	HW4	HW5	Q4	T3	HW	Quiz	Test	%
2		10	10	25	100	10	25	25	100	10	10	25	100				
3	Araceli	10	9	25	96	10	23	25	97	10	9	25	95				
4	Bill	9	9	23	92	10	22	24	95	10	9	24	90				
5	Callale	7	8	21	60	9	23	20	70	9	8	19	75				
6	Dirk	8	10	23	82	10	24	21	88	9	8	20	71				
7	Esther	10	10	24	91	9	22	23	98	10	10	24	94				
8																	
9																	

3. Finding Subtotals
   A. Click cell N2.
   B. Which cells contain the point values for homework? _____
   C. Use these cells to type a formula that computes the total possible homework score.
   D. Click cell O2.
   E. Which cells contain the point values for quizzes? _____
   F. Use these cells to type a formula that computes the total possible quiz points.
   G. Click cell P2.
   H. Which cells contain test scores? _____
   I. Use these cells to type a formula that computes the total possible test points.

4. Filling Down
   A. Select cells N2 through P7.
   B. Fill the formulas down so that computations are carried out for each student's data.

N	O	P	Q
HW	Quiz	Test	%
50	100	300	
48	98	288	
47	93	277	
41	83	205	
45	88	241	
49	93	283	

Activity 25: Weighted Grades *(cont.)*

5. Weighing Grades
   A. Click cell N9. Type *.25*. This indicates that homework counts for 25% of the grade. If only one decimal appears after you press <Enter>, use the **Increase Decimal** button from the Formatting Toolbar to adjust.
   B. Click cell O9. Type *.25*. This indicates that quizzes count for 25% of the grade.
   C. Click cell P9. Type *0.5*. This indicates that tests count for 50% of the grade.

6. Bold and center these values
   The key to successfully calculating weighted grades is to use the values that you just typed into cells N9, O9, and P9. You will have the spreadsheet calculate the percent of points earned in each of the three categories, and then multiply these percents by the decimal representing the weight of each item.
   A. Click cell Q3.
   B. Type *=$N$9*(N3/$N$2)+$O$9*(O3/$O$2)+$P$9*(P3/$P$2)*.
      N3/$N$2 finds the percent of homework points earned. When this is multiplied by $N$9 (.25 in this case), it calculates a numeric value between 0 and 100. This process is followed for quizzes and test, so there are three numeric values generated. The sum of these values is a grand total, that represents a value between 0 and 100. If grades are computed in a traditional way, values over 90 would correspond to an A, values between 80 and 90 would correspond to a B, etc. Recall that the dollar signs in the formula will ensure that the values in these cells are used in each calculation, even after the formula is filled to other cells. In the formula, $N$9 could be replaced with .25, as could $O$9. Use of cell labels allows you to change how factors are weighted without retyping a formula.
   C. Fill the formula down to cell Q7.
   D. Format cells Q3 to Q7 to be percents.

7. Finishing
   A. In the footer, type *Activity 25*, press <Enter>, and type *your name*.
   B. Go to **FILE** and select *Save*. Name the file *SS Act 25*.
   C. Print the spreadsheet in landscape format with the answers showing.
   D. Then print the spreadsheet in landscape format with the formulas showing.
   E. Go to **FILE** and select *Exit*.

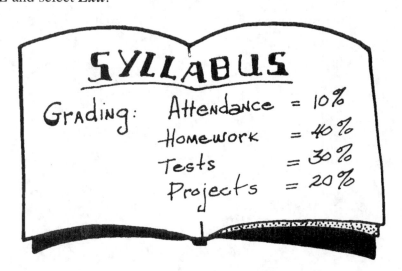

Activity 25: Time to Review and Extend

Check your answers on page 93.

1. What would the formula be to compute the weighted grades with information as depicted in the spreadsheet below?

	A	B	C	D
1		Homework	Quizzes	Tests
2		30	50	200
3	Student 1			
4	Student 2			
5	Student 3			
6				
7	Weight	0.1	0.25	0.65

_____

2. Explain what happens when certain factors are weighted into a grade.

_____

_____

Activity 26: Mary Jo's Budget

<u>Overview</u>: In this activity, you will create a budget spreadsheet to keep track of income and expenses on a monthly basis. Several of the functions and formulas from previous activities are used within the budget.

1. Open a new spreadsheet file.

2. Mary Jo wants to go on a weekend camping trip. The cost of this trip is $50.00. Can she afford to go? She decides to set up a budget to keep track of her income and expenses, which will help her determine if she has enough money to go on the trip. Set up your spreadsheet so it matches the one below.

	A	B	C	D	E	F	G	H
1	**Mary Jo's Budget**							
2								
3	**Income**	Jan	Feb	Mar	Apr	May	June	Total
4	Job	$40.00	$25.00	$20.00	$50.00	$20.00	$20.00	
5	Allowance	$10.00	$10.00	$10.00	$10.00	$10.00	$10.00	
6	Presents	$ -	$ -	$100.00	$ -	$ -	$25.00	
7	Month Total							
8								
9	**Expenses**	Jan	Feb	Mar	Apr	May	June	Total
10	CDs	$15.00	$ -	$30.00	$ -	$15.00	$15.00	
11	Movies	$5.00	$10.00	$5.00	$ -	$15.00	$ -	
12	Books	$7.50	$3.50	$ -	$ -	$10.00	$ -	
13	Miscellaneous	$15.00	$5.00	$10.50	$3.00	$5.00	$12.00	
14	Gifts	$ -	$20.00	$ -	$15.00	$10.00	$ -	
15	Eating Out	$10.00	$5.00	$5.00	$10.00	$12.00	$5.00	
16	Month Total							
17								
18	**Mary Jo's Savings**							

3. SUM Function
   A. What should be typed in cell H4 to add the contents of cells B4 through G4? _____
   B. Type this function and press <Enter>.
   C. Fill Down to cells H5 and H6.
   D. What should be typed in cell B7 to add the contents of cells B4 through B6? _____
   E. Type this function and press <Enter>.
   F. Fill Right to cells C7 through H7.
   G. What should be typed in cell H10 to add the contents of cells B10 through G10? _____
   H. Type this function and press <Enter>.
   I. Fill Down to cells H11 through H15.
   J. What should be typed in cell B16 to add the contents of cells B10 through B15? _____
   K. Type this function and press <Enter>.
   L. Fill Right to cells C16 through H16.

Activity 26: Mary Jo's Budget *(cont.)*

4. Monthly Savings
   A. What should be typed in cell B18 to calculate Mary Jo's savings for January?

   _____

   Hint: Look at the cell containing the total amount she earned for the month and the cell containing the total amount she spent for the month. Use these cell locations in the formula.
   B. Type this formula and press <Enter>.
   C. Fill Right to cells C18 through H18. The value in cell H18 is Mary Jo's total savings over the six month period.

5. Finishing
   A. In the footer, type *Activity 26*, press <Enter>, and type *your name*.
   B. Go to **FILE** and select *Save*. Name the file *SS Act 26*.
   C. Print the spreadsheet in landscape format with the answers showing.
   D. Then print the spreadsheet in landscape format with the formulas showing.
   E. Go to **FILE** and select *Exit*.

Activity 26: Time to Review and Extend

Answer the following questions. Check your responses with those on page 93.

1. Does Mary Jo have enough money in savings to go on the camping trip?

   _____

2. How were **Fill Down** and **Fill Right** helpful in completing this spreadsheet?

   _____

Activity 27: Mary Jo's Income Charts

Overview: You will expand upon the information that was included in the budget spreadsheet from Activity 26. You will add two charts to the budget data.

1. Open *Act 26 SS*. If you constructed the document, open it from your hard drive or floppy disk. If you skipped the activity, open it from the CD-ROM.

2. Go to **FILE** and select *Save As*. Name the file *SS Act 27*.

3. New Labels
   A. In cell A20, type *Income*.
   B. In cell A21, type *Expenses*.
   C. In cell A22, type *Savings*.

4. New Formulas
   A. Click cell B20. Type *=H7*.
   B. Click cell B21. Type *=H16*.
   C. Click cell B22. Type *=B20-B21*.
   D. If the values that appear in cells B20 through B22 are not formatted for currency, format them this way.

5. Make a Column Chart
   A. Select cells A20 through B22.
   B. Click the **Chart Wizard** button from the Standard Toolbar.
   C. Choose **Column** and make other formatting changes as desired.
   D. Click somewhere on the chart and drag it so it is positioned below cell A22.

6. Make a Pie Chart
   A. Select cells A21 through B22.
   B. Click the **Chart Wizard** button from the Standard Toolbar.
   C. Choose **Pie** and make other formatting changes as desired.
   D. Click somewhere on the chart and drag it so it is positioned next to the column chart.
   E. One or both of the charts may need to be resized so they can be placed next to each other on the spreadsheet.

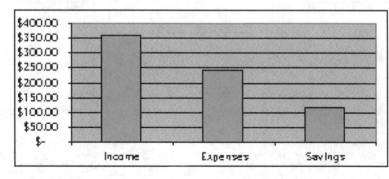 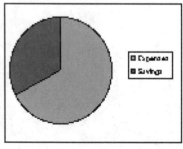

7. Finishing
   A. In the footer, type *Activity 27*, press <Enter>, and type *your name*.
   B. Go to **FILE** and select *Save*. Name the file *SS Act 27*.
   C. Print the spreadsheet in landscape format with the answers showing.
   D. Go to **FILE** and select *Exit*.

Activity 27: Time to Review and Extend

Answer the following questions. Check your responses with those on page 94.

1. In steps 4A and 4B, you typed formulas that did not include calculations. What did these formulas do? _____

    _____

2. What is the advantage of using the formulas in steps 4A and 4B rather than typing the numbers that appear in cells H7 and H16?

    _____

    _____

3. Study the two charts that you created. Do you think Mary Jo would be pleased if she saw these two charts? Why or why not?

    _____

    _____

Melinda Maury
17387 Lowell Avenue
Santa Monica, Ca. 96572

ABC Auto Insurance
16851 Winchester Blvd.
San Jose, Ca. 91642

Activity 28: My Budget

Overview: You will be provided with instructions to help you set up your own personal budget. As with Mary Jo's budget, you will use several functions and formulas to perform the calculations.

1. Set up a six month spreadsheet with the following headings. Substitute appropriate text for "source 1" and other cells. Depending on the number of income and expense sources that you have, you may need more or fewer rows than are displayed below. Your six month time period can run from January to June or July to December. Enter data; estimate where you need to.

	A	B	C	D	E	F	G	H
1	**Income**	Jan	Feb	Mar	Apr	May	June	Total
2	Source 1							
3	Source 2							
4	Source 3							
5	Grand Total							
6								
7								
8	**Expenses**	Jan	Feb	Mar	Apr	May	June	Total
9	Source 1							
10	Source 2							
11	Source 3							
12	Source 4							
13	Source 5							
14	Source 5							
15	Grand Total							
16								
17	Savings							

2. Add data to the spreadsheet as appropriate.

3. Add Functions and Formulas
   You might want to review pages 75–76 before proceeding.
   A. In cell H2, type the formula that will find the sum of source 1 income. Copy and paste this formula to the other cells that will use the equivalent calculation.
   B. In cell B5 (or equivalent on your spreadsheet), type the formula that will find the sum of the sources of income for January. Fill this formula to the other cells that will use the equivalent calculation.
   C. In cell H8 (or equivalent on your spreadsheet), type the formula that will find the sum of source 1 expenses. Fill this formula to the other cells that will use the equivalent calculation.
   D. In cell B14 (or equivalent on your spreadsheet), type the formula that will find the sum of January's expenses. Fill this formula to the other cells that will use the equivalent calculation.
   E. In cell B16 (or equivalent on your spreadsheet), type the formula that will calculate the amount of savings for the month. Fill this formula to the other cells that will use the equivalent calculation.

Activity 28: My Budget *(cont.)*

4. Finishing
   A. In the footer, type *Activity 28*, press <Enter>, and type *your name*.
   B. Go to **FILE** and select *Save*. Name the file *SS Act 28*.
   C. Print the spreadsheet in portrait format with the answers showing.
   D. Then print the spreadsheet in portrait format with the formulas showing.
   E. Go to **FILE** and select *Exit*.

Activity 28: Time to Review and Extend

Answer the following questions. Check your responses with those on page 94.

1. If you forgot one of your monthly expenses and needed to add a row to your spreadsheet, what would you do to make the row appear?

   _____

2. If you had $1,260.98 in your savings account at the beginning of the first month, what formula should be typed in the cell in which savings was calculated?

   _____

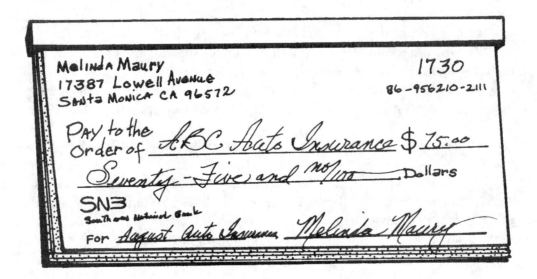

Activity 29: My Income Charts

<u>Overview</u>: In this activity, you will create a Column Chart and a Pie Chart as you examine your personal budget.

1. Open *SS Act 28*. If you constructed the document, open it from your hard drive or floppy disk. If you skipped the activity, open it from the CD-ROM.

2. Go to **FILE** and select *Save As*. Name the file *SS Act 29*.

3. New Labels
   A. In cell A31, type *Income*.
   B. In cell A32, type *Expenses*.
   C. In cell A33, type *Savings*.

4. New Formulas
   A. Click cell B31. Type the formula that will transfer your total income from the cell in which it is located on the spreadsheet.
   B. Click cell B32. Type the formula that will transfer your total expenses from the cell in which it is located on the spreadsheet.
   C. Click cell B33. Type *=B31-B32*.
   D. If the values that appear in cells B31 through B33 are not formatted for currency, format them this way.

5. Make a Column Chart
   A. Select cells A31 through B33.
   B. Click the **Chart Wizard** button and create a column chart using this data.
   C. Click somewhere on the chart and drag it so it is positioned below cell A33.

6. Make a Pie Chart
   A. Select cells A32 through B33.
   B. Click the **Chart Wizard** button and create a pie chart using this data.
   C. Click somewhere on the chart and drag it so it is positioned to the right of the column chart.

7. Finishing
   A. In the footer, type *Activity 29*, press <Enter>, and type *your name*.
   B. Go to **FILE** and select *Save*. Name the file *SS Act 29*.
   C. Print the spreadsheet in portrait format with the answers showing.
   D. Go to **FILE** and select *Exit*.

Activity 30: School Store

Overview: You will use the spreadsheet as a decision making tool in this activity. You will use various features of the spreadsheet as you set up a school store. You will use the spreadsheet to speculate the profit that will be generated from various selling prices of items.

Setting Up A Successful School Store

The student manager of the school store at Pleasantville Middle School must order supplies that will be available for students to purchase. The students of Pleasantville Middle School have voted to donate all of the school store's profits to charity, so the goal is to generate as much profit as possible.

The student manager orders supplies from McMurphy's Office Supply Catalog. These are the choices offered by McMurphy's, from which the manager may select up to 10 items to offer for sale at the school.

	A	B	C
1	Item	How Packaged	Cost Per Package
2	Glue Sticks	3 sticks per package	$7.95
3	Crayons-24 pack	1 package	$1.30
4	Glue	1 bottle	$1.75
5	Paper Clips	10 per package	$3.00
6	Scotch Tape	2 rolls per package	$1.30
7	White Out	2 bottles per package	$3.50
8	Looseleaf Paper	10 bundles per package	$5.00
9	2-inch binder	1 binder	$2.30
10	Floppy disks	100 per package	$40.00
11	Pencils	10 per package	$1.00
12	Pens	10 per package	$3.00
13	Highlighters	10 per package	$5.00
14	Stapler Kit	1 kit	$2.50
15	Eraser	3 per package	$1.50
16	Candy Bar	1 bar	$0.50
17	Scissors	3 per package	$5.00
18	Folders	10 per package	$5.00
19	Notebooks	6 per package	$4.80
20	Rulers	2 per package	$1.80
21	Poster Board	10 per package	$2.50

1. The student manager must figure out the cost to Pleasantville Middle School of each of the items available from McMurphy's Catalog. Set up a spreadsheet for this purpose. Format the spreadsheet so it looks like this.

	A	B	C	D
1	Item Name	Number of Items	Cost Per Package	Cost Per Item
2	Glue Sticks	3	$7.95	

2. Add the rest of the items to the spreadsheet, as well as the other relevant data. Column D will remain empty for now.

3. Use a formula in column D to compute the cost per item. What should the formula be for glue sticks? _____ Compare this response to the answer listed on page 94. Once you verify that it is correct, type this into cell D2.

Activity 30: School Store *(cont.)*

4. Fill the formula down to the other cells in the column.

5. Go to **FILE** and *Save* this spreadsheet as *SS Act 30a*.

6. Without closing *SS Act 30a*, open a new spreadsheet file. To do this, click the **NEW FILE** button from the Standard Toolbar.

7. Go to **FILE** and *Save* this spreadsheet as *SS Act 30b*.

8. Set up your spreadsheet like this.

	A	B	C	D	E	F	G	H	I
1			Total #	Stock		School		Income if All	
2			of Items	Available	Cost of	Selling	Total	Items Sell at	
3		Item	In Stock	Per Day	1 Item	Price	Cost	School Price	Profit
4	1								
5	2								
6	3								
7	4								
8	5								
9	6								
10	7								
11	8								
12	9								
13	10								

9. Fill in columns B and E using the information from *SS Act 30a*. To access this information again, click *SS Act 30b* in the Task Bar across the bottom of the screen.

Remember to choose items that you believe will generate a large profit for Pleasantville Middle School.

10. You need to order enough stock for one semester.
    - 500 students attend Pleasantville Middle School.
    - There are 50 days in a semester.
    - The School Store is only open during lunch, so that is 50 lunch periods of sales.
    Decide how many of each item you want to purchase, and enter these numbers into column C in *SS Act30b*.

11. Click cell D4 and type *=C4/50*. You use *50* in the formula because there are 50 lunch periods. Fill this formula to the other cells in column D. Experiment with numbers in column C until you are satisfied with your purchases.

Activity 30: School Store (cont.)

12. You obviously want to make a profit on each item that is sold. To do this, you must mark up the selling price of each item. The percent of markup may be different for each item. It is up to you to decide the best price for each supply. Supplies that are priced too high will not be purchased from the school store. Supplies that are priced too low will not generate as much profit as they could. You will need to type formulas into column F that represent the actual cost plus the percent markup for each item. Depending on the markup you decide upon, your formulas will look like this.

Candy Bars		
Markup	**Cost**	**Formula**
10%	$ 0.55	=0.5*1.10
25%	$ 0.62	=0.5*1.25
50%	$ 0.75	=0.5*1.50
100%	$ 1.00	=0.5*2.00

13. Why does the formula contain 1.10, even though the markup is just 10%?_____

14. Click cell G4. Build a formula that shows the Total Cost for each item. Use cell locations to build this formula. Fill this formula through cell G13.

15. Click cell H4. Build a formula that shows how much money would be generated if every item in the school store sold at the selling price. Use cell locations to build this formula. Fill this formula down through cell H13.

16. Click cell G14. Use the SUM formula to calculate the Total Cost of the products.

17. Click cell H14. Use the SUM formula to calculate the Total Profit from the products if all items were sold.

18. Click cell I14. Use a formula to figure out how much money Pleasantville Middle School will give to charity. Bold this answer.

19. Finishing
    A. In the footer, type *Activity 30b*, press <Enter>, and type *your name*.
    B. Go to **FILE** and select *Save*.
    C. Print the spreadsheet in landscape format with the answers showing.
    D. Then print the spreadsheet in landscape format with the formulas showing.
    E. Go to **FILE** and select *Exit*.

Activity 30: Time to Review and Extend

1. Using Sheet 1 and Sheet 2.

   A. Go to **FILE** and select *Open*. Select *SS Act 30a*.
   B. Go to **FILE** and select *Open*. Select *SS Act 30b*.
   C. In *SS Act 30b*, select the contents of cells A1 through I14.
   D. Go to **EDIT** and select *Copy*.
   E. In the Task Bar across the bottom of the screen, click on **SS Act 30a**.
   F. Click the **Sheet 2** tab and then click cell A1.
   G. Go to **EDIT** and select *Paste*.
   H. Save this file. It will be saved as one file that contains two sheets. If we had followed these steps in Activity 30, there would not have been a need to save *SS Act 30a* <u>and</u> *SS Act 30b*. *SS Act 30a* now contains all of the information.

2. Give two examples of how a business would use a spreadsheet.

   _____

   _____

Classroom Integration Ideas

Spreadsheets can be very useful software programs because they allow students to focus on curricular content rather than on mathematical calculations. In fact, National and State standards often include technology-related goals and objectives that spreadsheet programs can address. The types of activities for which students would use a spreadsheet would, in large part, depend upon student familiarity with computers and spreadsheets, student understanding of mathematical concepts, and student grade level.

Below, several "starter" ideas are provided just to get you thinking about the vast realm of possibilities. These ideas are grouped around science, social studies, language arts, and mathematics.

Science

The relationship between science and mathematics is very strong, so there are a lot of opportunities where students can use spreadsheets in the science curriculum.

1. Students can store information about planets, such as circumference, distance from the sun, density, etc. Students can graph the information and also perform calculations within the spreadsheet.
2. Students could track observations of plant growth. Students can record plant height on a daily basis and chart this information.
3. Primary students can track and chart the number of teeth they lose per month as a class.
4. Students can track the boiling point and freezing point of various substances.
5. A spreadsheet allows students to examine the predator-prey relationship, and how animal populations can be altered if one part of the relationship is out-of-balance.
6. Spreadsheets can help students compare physical properties of rocks and other substances by mathematically adjusting qualities based on one characteristic. For example, if students collected data for several rocks in a collection, they can compare based on the degree of characteristics if the observed rocks were all the same mass.
7. Students can use spreadsheets to convert from Fahrenheit to Celsius to Kelvin degrees.
8. Formulas that typically are solved either manually or with a calculator can be solved by using a spreadsheet. Students can set up spreadsheet columns to represent the variables in a formula, and then have the program compute the result.
9. Position, velocity, and acceleration are related. Students can record information in a spreadsheet to be able to see and understand this relationship.

Social Science

Spreadsheets can be used well in a social science curriculum because the chart feature allows students to make comparisons. In addition, teachers can set up simulations involving numerical data that may otherwise be difficult to set up.

1. Teachers can create simulations of historical periods. Students use a spreadsheet to record and compute pertinent information. Students make decisions based on their understanding, and then see how their decisions influence other events.
2. Students can keep track of fictitious stock purchases, and track prices. Students can also be asked to use a spreadsheet in understanding the stock market crash.
3. Population growth in a city, state, or country can be examined using a spreadsheet. Students can examine trends and make predictions based on their analyses.
4. A spreadsheet is a useful tool to help students understand population density.
5. The Mayan number system was a base 20 system. Students can learn about the culture by using a spreadsheet to compare Mayan numbers with our Hindu-Arabic system.
6. When various presidential cabinets are explored, spreadsheets can be developed to compare expenditures in the national budget. This allows students to control for inflation.
7. Principles of the Free Market Economy (supply and demand) can be explored using a spreadsheet.

Classroom Integration Ideas *(cont.)*

Language Arts

Language Arts does not have the numerical focus found in other subject areas, so spreadsheets will likely not be used as much as in mathematics, science, and social studies. However, there are still some possibilities.

1. Keep a chart of the number of pages read by student on a weekly or monthly basis.
2. Have students explore the number of active and passive verbs in sentences of different document types (fiction, non-fiction, newspapers).
3. Students can develop charts with the assistance of spreadsheet programs that can be incorporated into material that they write and/or present verbally.

Mathematics

There is an obvious relationship between spreadsheets and the mathematics curriculum. There are many ways in which the spreadsheet can be used. This is just a small sample.

1. Spreadsheets can help students understand the relationship between fractions, decimals, and percents.
2. Primary students can use a teacher-generated spreadsheet that helps them self-assess whether they have correctly made change for a purchase.
3. Percent of increase and decrease can be examined using a spreadsheet.
4. Any word problem that would be typically solved using trial and error could be solved using formulas within a spreadsheet.
5. Geometry concepts such as perimeter, area, and volume can be explored using spreadsheets.
6. Real-life mathematical concepts such as loans can be studied through spreadsheets.

More Ideas

Teacher Created Resources has several resources available for purchase that can provide you with additional ideas regarding ways that spreadsheets can be used across the curriculum. Check the catalog or Web site frequently to learn about new titles that might be helpful.

These products are currently available:

*Microsoft Excel for Terrified Teachers**
*Microsoft Excel Simple Projects (Primary)**
*Microsoft Excel Simple Projects (Intermediate)**
*Microsoft Excel Simple Projects (Challenging)**
            *These same titles are also available for *AppleWorks (ClarisWorks).*

TechTools Resource Kit for Microsoft Excel
    Turn to this kit for the answers to technical questions, for creative project ideas, and for those important extras that turn mundane reports into spectacular printed documents. In it you'll find 100 "How-to" Cards that give illustrated step-by-step instructions. Both beginning and advanced software users will find the answers to their questions. For ideas on how to use the software as a teaching tool, look inside the Teacher's Resource Notebook. You'll find detailed plans for 60 project-based lessons. For added interest (and fun!), check out the Multimedia CD.

Answers to Activity Questions

Page 6
IV

Page 7
65,536
B) IV65536

Page 8
1B) 1234
1C) 1234
2A) HI
2B) HI

Page 9
Activity A) *Answers will vary* Dear Mom, I am writing to you today to describe a spreadsheet program. To start the program, you go to START, Programs, and select *Microsoft Excel*. You will see a new grid that is made up of columns and rows. The box where each column and row intersect is called a cell. I always know which is the active cell because its label is displayed in the active cell address. If I need to change any of the formulas, numbers, or labels that I have typed into my spreadsheet, I can do that in the Entry Bar. After all of that, I just have to remember to save the document.

Activity B) *Answers will vary.* To begin using the *Microsoft Excel* spreadsheet program, you go to START, Programs, and select *Microsoft Excel*. All of the horizontal and vertical lines that you see when you open the program are part of the grid. Information that is listed vertically in a spreadsheet program is entered in a column. Information that is listed horizontally in a spreadsheet program is entered in a row. The place where a row and column intersect is called a cell. When you click on a cell, it is defined as the active cell. This label of every cell is called the cell address. If you need to change something that you have entered into one of the cells, you click the Entry Bar. Calculations in a spreadsheet are entered as formulas. You can also enter numbers and labels into spreadsheet cells. After entering information into a spreadsheet, you should save the document.

Page 12
8C) 403 was displayed, which is the result of 389 + 14
9C) 679 was displayed, which is the result of 936-257
10C) 6500 was displayed, which is the result of 450*8

Page 13
11C) 927 was displayed, which is the result of 278,100 divided by 300.

Page 14
1) *Answers will vary.* A program that allows the computer to perform calculations.
2) labels, numbers, and formulas
3) equal sign
4) =A1+A2+A3
5) =A1*B1*C1

Page 16
G=SUM(B3:B6); =SUM(C5:F5)

Answers to Activity Questions *(cont.)*

Page 17
5) =SUM(C1:C9)

Page 18
Review 1) =B2+B3+B4+B5+B6+B7+B8+B9+B10
Review 2) The SUM function allows a range of cells to be specified rather than having to manually type each cell label into the formula.
Review 3) =SUM(K1:K250)

Page 19
4E) 141
4F) =A2+B2
4G) The cell labels in the formulas automatically adjust depending on the row.

Page 21
Review 1) It copies a function or formula to additional cells in a column.
Review 2) If you have already typed a function or formula and want to use it repeatedly, the Fill Down command eliminates unnecessary retyping.
Review 3) It changes the cell labels automatically based on the row to which it will be applied.

Page 22
3) =sum(B1:B3)
4) The Bs in the formula need to change to the label that represents each column.

Page 23
1) The Fill Right command takes a function or formula from one cell, copies it, adjusts the labels based on the new column, and then pastes to selected cells.
2) Fill Right. The Fill command can be used to copy and paste text and formulas.

Page 25
5C) *Answers will vary.*
5E) The formula multiplied the number of backpacks times the price of each one.
6C) *Answers will vary.*
6E) The formula multiplied the number of pairs of shoes times the price per pair.
7B) =B4*D4
8B) =B6*C6
8C) Yes, this formula is correct.

Page 26
10C) *Answers will vary.*
10E) You are correct, hopefully!
10F) =Sum(D2:D9)
11B) =D10*.06
13B) =D10+D11 or =sum(D10:D11)

Page 27
3A) *Answers will vary.*
3B) $89.85
3D) $119.85
3E) The change occurred because the formula used to compute the jacket total was =C4*D4. Because labels were used in the formula, the adjustment was automatically made when a new price was entered.

Answers to Activity Questions *(cont.)*

<u>Page 27</u>
4A) *Answers will vary.*
4B) $7.14
4D) $10.71
4E) The change occurred because the formula used to compute the paper total was =C5*D5. Because labels were used in the formula, the adjustment was automatically made when a new item total was entered.
5A) *Answers will vary.*
5B) $297.42
5C) $17.85
5D) $315.27

<u>Page 28</u>
5F) $298.59
5G) 17.92
5H) $316.51.
Review 1) The changes were automatic because cell labels were used in the formulas. If numbers had been used in the formulas, then the adjustments would not have been made.
Review 2) No changes would have been made to the subtotal, tax, or grand total because the formula would not have resulted in any number changes in the spreadsheet.

<u>Page 31</u>
9A) =B4*C4 would be used for the first item, all others would follow that pattern except adjust for the row number
9E) =SUM(D4:D12) <u>or</u> =D4+D5+D6+D7+D8+D9+D10+D11+D12
9G) =D14/30
9H) By using the label for the grand total in the formula, the student contribution will be adjusted if changes are made to the items purchased for the party.
9J) The spreadsheet allows you to make changes to cost and number of items purchased. If the goal is to keep student contributions less than a certain total, the spreadsheet helps you adjust as necessary.

<u>Page 33</u>
5) =B9*C9
6) =sum(D4:D14) <u>or</u> =D4+D5+D6+D7+D8+D9+D10+D11+D12+D13+D14
7) =D15-60

<u>Page 34</u>
1) Change the quantities purchased, buy items that are less expensive, and eliminate items that are not necessary.
2) See *SS Act 9a* on the CD-ROM.
3) See *SS Act 9b* on the CD-ROM.
4) See *SS Act 9c* on the CD-ROM.
5) A spreadsheet allows you to manipulate data to see results of various changes.

<u>Page 36</u>
7) =B4*C4
8) =SUM(D2:D11) <u>or</u> =D2+D3+D4+D5+D6+D7+D8+D9+D10+D11
Review) If you had not used the cell labels, the grand total would not have adjusted as you changed the quantity or value of the items you would purchase.

Answers to Activity Questions *(cont.)*

<u>Page 38</u>

A) 20; multiply first, then divide, then add.

B) 28; Add 8+6 first, Divide 4/2 second, and then multiply 14 by 2.

C) 18; Take 4 and square it first, then subtract 8-6, and last add the result (2) to 16.

D) 4; Subtract 8-6 first, divide 4/2 second, and then take 2 (from the 8-6) to the second power.

E) 14; Multiply 8*6 first, then divide 48 by 4 and lastly, add 2 to this answer.

<u>Page 39</u>

5) =A6/(B6-C6)/D6 is one possible answer, =A7/(B7-C7)-D7 is another, other possibilities may exist.

6) *Answers will vary.*

Review 1) Parentheses are first, then powers, then multiplication and division from left to right, and last addition and subtraction from left to right.

Review 2) Order of Operations is important because answers of mathematical expressions are dependent upon the consistent application of these rules. Different answers would result if not followed.

<u>Page 40</u>

4) =B7*(B5+B6)

5) =B5*B3+B6*B4

<u>Page 41</u>

8) =B10-B9

Review 1) $545.50

Review 2) *Answers will vary.*

<u>Page 43</u>

Review) It would be a good idea here to use specific combinations of numbers for adult and children tickets, and various estimates of the number of people who would attend the event based on this data.

<u>Page 46</u>

Review 1) The chart clearly depicts that students overwhelmingly favor cookies as an after-school treat.

Review 2) You use a column chart when you want to compare numerical quantities.

Review 3) *Answers will vary*, examples may be population data from different states or countries, depth of bodies of water, votes by political party on a law or bill.

Review 4) *Answers will vary*, examples include number of descriptive words per paragraph in various books, number of grammar errors by gender on a quiz.

<u>Page 48</u>

5) The chart automatically changed based on the new data.

<u>Page 49</u>

Review 1) It would be useful to examine the foods that are not listed as favorites by either boys or girls. Pizza has a pretty equal distribution, so that might be an indication that it would be acceptable to members of both genders.

Review 2) You can change data in your spreadsheet without having to re-create the graph.

Review 3) *Answers will vary*, examples might be the number of tardies before and after a new reading program, the number of participants in various sports by gender, and the number of students involved in various school clubs.

Answers to Activity Questions *(cont.)*

Page 54
Review 1) Without knowing all of the circumstances, only speculations can be made. One possibility is that there was a midweek lull and as a result, people were looking for something to add a little spark to things. Other possibilities could be related to weather or a special event that was going on that day.
Review 2) Again, it is speculative. It is possible that by Thursday, people are looking ahead to the weekend and trying to save some money for that. It could also have related to temperature.
Review 3) Overall, the profits of Annie and Billy seem pretty balanced. Annie has higher profits on three days, but Billy's profits were higher on two days.
Review 4) Annie makes a total of $75.50 while Billy earns $72.50. There is not much difference between the two.

Page 56
Review 1) In general, middle school students are not getting enough sleep. Parents should make an effort to try to get their middle school-aged kids to bed earlier.
Review 2) Consider beginning the school day a little later in the morning so that students can sleep longer.
Review 3) Charting pet preferences, relating pie charts to fractions and percents.

Page 59
Review 1) You would use a pie chart when you want to visually compare parts of a whole.
Review 2) The Student Council could use a pie chart to chart student interest in possible mascots, student lunch preferences, and grade distribution by quarter.
Review 3) The numbers would be 17, 8, 3, 2 in that order. But 17 would be listed with blue eyes while 8 would be paired with brown eyes. This is not consistent with the actual data pairings.

Page 61
Review 1) Billy gradually increased his average over time. He has since encountered a plateau.
Review 2) *Answers may vary.* About 250. He is on a plateau right now–his scores have evened out. His average is already very high, so it will be difficult for him to increase it.
Review 3) If you want to look at data over a time period.
Review 4) Accuracy on timed math tests, scores on timed math tests.

Page 63
Review 1) Profits decreased gradually during the year in both 2000 and 2001. Students tend to buy more supplies at the beginning of the school year.
Review 2) The store manager needs to be sure to have enough supplies on hand to meet the demand early in the year.
Review 3) A line chart could be used to track temperature in two beakers as they are heated or cooled, a line chart could be used to track the distance of two planets from the earth or sun.

Page 64
5) The spreadsheet found the mean of the numbers in column B.

Page 66
Review 1) =AVERAGE(C3:Y3)
Review 2) The computer adds the numbers in the range of selected cells and then divides by how many cells are in the range.
Review 3) =SUM(B1:B10)/10
Review 4) The formula listed in Review 3 requires that you count the number of entries in the selected range. The AVERAGE function does the counting for you.

Answers to Activity Questions *(cont.)*

Page 67

8C) It is not meaningful to compare the students' averages to the whole. Column charts or line charts would be better visual representations of the data.

Review 1) Because all of the tests equal 100 points. If that was not the case, the AVERAGE function could not be used to compute the percent. With this data, the points for each of the tests are the same as the percentages for each of the tests.

Review 2) Without pressing <CTRL>, the two non-adjacent columns could not have been selected.

Page 68

Review L) It added extra bars to represent the unhidden rows.

Review M) You can still see all the content.

Page 70

9A) F3

9B) F2

9C) =F3/F2

10B) =F3/F2

10C) yes

10D) =F4/F3

10E) no

10I) yes

Page 71

Review 1) Not all of the point values were out of 100, which meant that the points and percents were not the same.

Review 2) The dollar signs allowed a cell label to stay the same when a Fill was performed.

Review 3) Whenever you want data from a specific cell copied to other cells in the spreadsheet.

Page 72

3B) B2, C2, F2, J2, and K2

3E) D2, G2, H2, and L2

3H) E2, I2, and M2

Page 74

Review 1) =$B$7*(B3/$B$2)+$C$7*(C3/$C$2)+$D$7*(D3/$D$2) <u>or</u>
.1*(B3/$B$2)+.25*(C3/$C$2)+.65*(D3/$D$2)

Review 2) The percent of the student's total in each weighted category is multiplied by the weight of the factor. All of the factors are then added together for a result between 0 and 100. The resulting total corresponds to a letter grade.

Page 75

3A) =SUM(B4:G4)

3D) =SUM(B4:B6)

3G) =SUM(B10:G10)

3J) =SUM(B10:B15)

Page 76

4A) =B7-B16

Review 1) Yes

Review 2) The use of the fill commands greatly decreased the number of functions and formulas that would otherwise have had to be typed manually.

Answers to Activity Questions *(cont.)*

<u>Page 78</u>
Review 1) They copied the value from one cell to another cell in the spreadsheet.
Review 2) If you change numbers in the spreadsheet, these formulas will automatically be updated in cells B20 through B22. In addition, the chart will be updated as well.
Review 3) It depends on Mary Jo's goals. Her expenses are much higher than her savings, so that might be something that she would like to change. On the other hand, she might be satisfied just to have any savings at all.

<u>Page 80</u>
Review 1) Click the row number below the spot where you would like the new one placed. Then go to **FORMAT** and select *Insert Cells.*
Review 2) =1260.98+B5-B14 (or the equivalent formula using the cell labels that are consistent with the data in your spreadsheet.

<u>Page 82</u>
3) =C2/B2

<u>Page 84</u>
13) If you only use .10 in the formula, you will need to go back and add this product back to the original amount ($.50). If you use 1.10, the formula will start with $.50 and then add an additional 10% to that.

<u>Page 85</u>
Review 2) Businesses use spreadsheets to keep track of profits and losses, keep track of inventory, and to track market demand.

Glossary

Absolute Cell References—Cell references within a formula that do not adjust when copied from one cell to another. The dollar sign is used to specify absolute cell references.

Active cell—The cell in your worksheet that has been selected. The active cell has a bolder gridline around it. The active cell's address appears in the Name Box above the worksheet.

AutoFill—A *Microsoft Excel* feature that allows you to quickly apply the contents of one cell to another cell or a range of selected cells.

AutoSum—A *Microsoft Excel* function that automatically identifies and adds ranges of cells in your worksheet.

Button—A clickable "hot spot" on your screen. Clicking a button initiates an action in *Microsoft Excel*, such as save or print.

Cancel button—A button to the left of the formula bar that allows you to cancel the contents of the active cell.

CD-ROM—Compact disc-read only memory stores files in digital form. It can be accessed to open files just like your floppy disk drive and hard drive.

CD-ROM drive—The mechanism used to access files on your CD-ROM. The CD-ROM drive is typically designated as drive D:\ on your computer system.

Cell—The rectangular-shaped area on a worksheet that is created by the intersection of a column and a row. The cell is where you enter and store data in a worksheet.

Cell address—The name of a cell that is determined by the intersection of a column and a row. The address of the cell that is formed by the intersection of column A and row 8 is A8.

Cell grid—The lines on your worksheet that separate the columns and rows.

Click—The action you perform when you push a button on the mouse to position your cursor, select an item, or activate a *Microsoft Excel* feature.

Close—A drop down menu item that puts away a workbook file you are no longer using.

Close button—The small square button with the X in it at the top of your screen. Clicking on this button closes the *Microsoft Excel* program.

Close window button—The small square button with the X in it at the end of the menu bar. It is identical to and located just below the close button. Clicking on this button closes the workbook you are no longer using.

Column—In a worksheet, the vertical spaces with headings A, B, C, and so on.

Command line—A place in a *Microsoft Excel* window where you type information, such as a file name.

Copy—The process of selecting numbers and/or text and placing them in memory for pasting in another location. When you copy, the original numbers and/or text you selected remains on the screen.

Cursor—The symbol displayed on the computer screen (a blinking bar, an I-beam, an arrowhead, or other icon) that indicates where your next keystroke will appear in your worksheet.

Cut—To remove text or numbers from the active cell or range of selected cells in a worksheet.

Default—How the settings are automatically. For example, the default column width in a *Microsoft Excel* worksheet is 8.43 points.

Delete—To remove text or numbers from the active cell or range of selected cells in a worksheet.

Delete key—A key on your keyboard that erases items on your screen. When you press the delete key, the text or numbers to the right of the cursor are cleared. If text or numbers in a cell or range of cells is selected, when you press the delete key, the entire highlighted area is cleared.

Deselect—After a range of cells has been selected (highlighted) and worked with, clicking in an unselected area of the worksheet to deactivate the original selection or highlighting.

Dialog box—A box that appears on your screen that prompts you to provide some type of input, such as text or values, or that prompts you to make a selection or click a button.

Drag—When you move the mouse while holding down the mouse button (usually the left) to select a range of cells.

Enter button—A button to the left of the formula bar that you click to accept the contents of the active cell, such as a formula.

Enter key—A key on your keyboard that you press when you want your cursor to move the next line. Pressing enter also indicates that you have made a selection or accepted a formula. It is the same as the Return key.

Exit—A drop-down menu item that allows you to quit the *Microsoft Excel* program when selected.

File—A document that is stored on your computer, floppy diskette, or CD-ROM. In *Microsoft Excel*, a file is also known as a workbook.

Filename—The name you give a file upon saving it.

Fill down—A *Microsoft Excel* feature that allows you to copy information in an active cell to another cell or range of cells you have selected vertically.

Fill right—A *Microsoft Excel* feature that allow you to copy information in an active cell to another cell or range of cells you have selected horizontally.

Floppy disk drive—The mechanism used to access files on your floppy diskette. The floppy disk drive is typically designated as drive A:\ on your computer system.

Font—The type face of letters formed as you enter text in your worksheet, such as Helvetica and Arial.

Formatting—Working with the attributes of components of the worksheet on your screen, such as resizing, bolding, and centering the text.

Formatting toolbar—A series of drop-down menus and buttons above your worksheet that allows you change the type face, type size, type attributes, text and number alignment, and more.

Formula—A combination of numbers and symbols used to express a calculation. The formula =SUM(A1:A6) tells *Microsoft Excel* to add the numbers in cells A1 through A6.

Formula bar—A command line above the worksheet where text, numbers, and formulas are entered into a worksheet.

Function—A drop-down menu item and a button on the standard toolbar that allows you to select a formula that you wish to apply to data

Glossary *(cont.)*

in your worksheet.

Hard disk drive—A high-speed, high-density alternative to the floppy disk drive. So called because the platter on which the data is stored is rigid.

Hardware—The parts of your computer that you can see and touch.

Headings—The identifying letters and numbers for columns and rows. Columns are identified by the letters A, B, C, and so on. Rows are identified by the numbers 1, 2, 3, and so on.

Highlight—When the mouse is dragged over the cells in a worksheet, they become highlighted. The highlighting indicates that the cells are selected and ready to be manipulated.

Icon—A small image on your computer screen used to represent a specific program or to initiate an action in *Microsoft Excel*.

Input—Data that comes into the computer from some kind of input device such as a disk drive, the keyboard, or a microphone.

Insert—To enter text or numbers at the position of the cursor or cell pointer.

Internet—An international web of computer networks.

Justification—Alignment of text or numbers within a worksheet cell. The alignment may be left-justified, centered, or right-justified.

Label—The identifying name that reflects the information contained in a column or row in a worksheet. A column label may be Name. A row label may be *Date*.

Landscape—A screen orientation where the longer side of a worksheet or chart extends from side to side. For typical documents landscape orientation is typically 11" x 8.5". It is the opposite of portrait orientation which is 8.5" x 11".

Launch—To open a software program, such as *Microsoft Excel*, so you can use it.

Legend—An explanation of the data series on a chart.

Menu—A list of available options.

Menu bar—The set of menu items, such as File, Edit, View, Insert, etc., displayed at the top of the screen in *Microsoft Excel*.

Monitor—The screen you use to display the *Microsoft Excel* worksheet that is being processed by your computer.

Mouse—A small, mechanical piece of computer hardware that you roll on your desk and click to control where text and numbers will be placed in your worksheet, as well as which items are selected on your screen.

Mouse button—One of two or three spots on the mouse that you depress or click to make a selection.

Name box—A display area above your worksheet that shows the cell address of the active cell or range of cells.

New—A drop-down menu item and a button on the standard toolbar that allows you to open a new workbook file.

Open—A drop-down menu item and a button on the standard toolbar that allows you to open an existing workbook file.

Paste—To insert text or numbers that were selected and copied into an active cell or range of cells.

Pointer arrow—The arrow that appears on the screen and moves when the mouse is moved.

Portrait orientation—A screen orientation where the shorter side of a worksheet or chart extends from side to side. For typical documents portrait orientation is 8.5" x 11". It is the opposite of landscape orientation which is 11" x 8.5".

Print—To make a hard copy of a worksheet or other document.

Printer—The device you use for producing a hard copy of your *Microsoft Excel* worksheet.

Relative Cell References—Cell references within a formula that adjust when copied from one cell to another.

Return key— A key on your keyboard that you press when you want your cursor to move the next line. Pressing return also indicates that you have made a selection or accepted a formula. It is the same as the Enter key.

Rows—In a worksheet, the horizontal spaces with the headings 1, 2, 3, and so on.

Save—The pull-down menu item or button on the standard toolbar that allows you to store your workbook on the hard drive or your floppy diskette.

Select—Identifying a cell or range of cells so that you can apply some type of action, such as copy, delete, or bold.

Sheet tabs—Tabs you see at the bottom of your workbook file. The tabs are labeled Sheet1, Sheet2, Sheet3, and so on, although you can rename the tabs, giving them more meaningful names. They represent the worksheets within the workbook.

Shift/Tab—A key combination on your keyboard that allows you to move the active cell to the left.

Spreadsheet—An application program, such as *Microsoft Excel*, that appears as a ledger and allows you to enter text and numerical data in rows and columns.

Standard toolbar— A series of drop-down menus and buttons above your worksheet that allows you open, save, print, and preview workbook files. It also allows you to quickly cut, copy, and paste selected areas of your worksheet and more.

Tab key—A navigation key on your keyboard that allows you to move your active cell one cell to the right.

Template—A way to save a workbook file so that you can use its structure over and over again. When you create or open a template file, always rename it so that the original file remains intact.

Text—The letters or words that you type into a cell in a *Microsoft Excel* worksheet.

Window—An enclosed area on your screen that is an independent object for data-processing purposes. Several windows can be open at the same time, enable you to easily switch from one task to another.

Word processing program—A productivity software application used primarily for working with written communication, such as text.

Word wrap—A characteristic of the *Microsoft Excel* program that allows text that extends beyond the right side of the cell to move to the beginning of a new line within the cell.

Workbook—A *Microsoft Excel* file that contains individual worksheets. It is also sometimes called a spreadsheet file.

Worksheet—A "page" within a *Microsoft Excel* workbook that contains columns, rows, and cells.